YOU CAN DO IT

OTHER BOOKS BY MARCUS RASHFORD

You Are a Champion
Written with Carl Anka

The Breakfast Club Adventures:
The Beast Beyond the Fence
Written with Alex Falase-Koya

MARCUS RASHFORD

YOU CAN DO IT

HOW TO FIND YOUR VOICE AND MAKE A DIFFERENCE

Written with Carl Anka

With contributions from Shannon Weber

MACMILLAN CHILDREN'S BOOKS

First published 2022 by Macmillan Children's Books
a division of Macmillan Publishers Limited
The Smithson, 6 Briset Street, London EC1M 5NR
EU representative: Macmillan Publishers Ireland Ltd, 1st Floor,
The Liffey Trust Centre, 117–126 Sheriff Street Upper
Dublin 1, D01 YC43
Associated companies throughout the world
www.panmacmillan.com

ISBN 978-1-5290-9705-4

1 3 5 7 9 8 6 4 2

A CIP catalogue record for this book is available from the British Library.

Designed by Janene Spencer

Printed and bound by CPI Group (UK) Ltd, Croydon CR0 4YY

TO EVERY YOUNG PERSON WHO WANTS
TO MAKE A DIFFERENCE IN THE WORLD.

FOR MY COMMUNITY AND EVERYONE WHO
HAS PLAYED A ROLE IN MY JOURNEY.

CONTENTS

HELLO FRIEND!

MY NAME IS MARCUS RASHFORD AND I'M A PROFESSIONAL FOOTBALLER FOR MANCHESTER UNITED AND THE ENGLAND NATIONAL TEAM. I'm also an author now, which feels weird because I only started reading for fun in my late teenage years! I really enjoy working on books — you may have read my first book, *You Are a Champion*, which was all about showing kids (and adults) how to be the best they can be.

For me, a good book can be like a key that unlocks doors in your mind. It can teach you new things and show you new ways to look at the world. So in *You Are a Champion*, I decided to collect as much of the stuff I've learned over my years playing football, championing others and doing all sorts of other things, and put it all in one place for someone else — like you — to enjoy.

I really enjoyed writing *You Are a Champion*, and it was amazing to see the reactions of so many people who read it. And if you've already read that book, I'd just like to say thank you one more time. I hope you liked it, and I hope it helps you on your journey through life.

A lot of people have asked me questions about things that I described in that book, particularly the anti-food-poverty project I did across much of 2020. All of these questions, and hearing that people wanted to know more, inspired me to start thinking about what I could write next. I thought that if *You Are a Champion* was all about showing people that they are filled to the brim with potential, then my next book – this book that you are holding right now – should be about showing people how they can use their talents to do something amazing. To make a difference in the world around them.

I've been really fortunate in my life. I get to use my football talents nearly every day for a club and a country that I love. I've also been able to take some of my skills for working in a team to things away from football, like my anti-food-poverty project.

Football and helping others are two of my biggest passions in life, and with this book I want to show you that your passions can lead you to incredible places, and to meet the most incredible people.

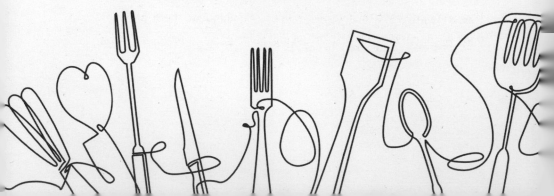

The Covid-19 pandemic was a difficult time for a lot of people. We all had to stay at home under lockdown in early 2020, and it got me thinking about the millions of households in the country who might need some help putting food on the table. As you'll learn later in this book, my mum often needed a little help when I was a child, and I started to wonder how I might go about helping the next generation who were having a tough time. That process set me on a journey that led me to work with some inspiring and generous people who all grouped together to help millions of families in the UK. I'll tell you more about all that later on in this book, but what I want you to know right now is this:

FOLLOWING UP ON THE THINGS YOU CARE ABOUT CAN ONE DAY HELP TO CHANGE THE WORLD.

Everyone in this world has their own unique journey in life, and your passions will help you navigate your future. They can help you to find something you believe in and to find your voice, and can show you how you can make a real difference — both to you, your friends and, ultimately, the community around you.

How someone uses their voice is completely unique to them, and I don't want you to think that I'm asking you to go out there and change the world right now, all by yourself. Finding your voice can be as simple as being a bit more confident in sharing something you enjoy, or standing up for a friend who is in need. Making a difference can be as small as recycling a can of cola after you've drunk it. Even the smallest changes can make the biggest difference — small steps lead to something amazing. And you don't have to do it all by yourself.

As I've got older and more and more incredible things have happened in my life, I've realised that everyone has the potential within them to do brilliant things, but that their brilliance has much more impact when they use it to work together with other people.

SO THAT'S WHAT THIS BOOK IS ALL ABOUT:
WORKING TOGETHER.

This book is called *You Can Do It*. It follows on from my book *You Are a Champion*, but in this book when I say YOU, I mean not just one person but LOADS of people at the same time. Loads of different champions, all working together to take care of each other and of causes they find are important to them.

The book you are holding is going to be full of advice about how you can look after yourself and find your place in the world. It's also going to show you that the best place for you in the world is working as part of a team.

THIS BOOK IS ALL **YOU**.
YOUR GROUP. YOUR FAMILY.
YOUR FRIENDS. YOUR
CLASSMATES. YOUR COMMUNITY.
YOUR WORLD. YOUR TEAM.

Within you right now is the most incredible energy that could one day make a huge difference in this world, but in order to do that, you're going to need to get a little help from others.

You're also going to have to help other people.

This book is my way of helping you on your journey to finding your voice and the things that are important to you. It's a big wide world out there, and the things that you like and that inspire *you* may not be the same as for everyone else.

That's ok. I don't want you to worry. There's no such thing as normal, and what's important is that you feel confident, cared for, and are happy on whatever journey you might be on.

I also want you to know that because there's no such thing as normal, you don't need to be scared or weirded out by seeing anyone doing anything a bit different from what you do. Part of working in a group and living in a community is realising that everyone is a bit different, and you will learn to embrace that difference and use it for the greater good of everyone.

BECAUSE THAT'S WHO I WOULD REALLY LIKE YOU TO THINK ABOUT WHEN READING THIS BOOK: EVERYONE.

Another thing I really like about books is how there is nearly always someone else who has read the same book as you. Take a moment and think about that. There is someone out there in the world who has read the exact same sentence that you are reading right now. You might meet them one day. Or you might not. But I would like you to think about that other person from time to time. Think about what their hopes might be, what their dreams are, and the community they might be a part of.

Then, I want you to have a think about what might happen if you worked together on something you both care about loads.

Because that's where the magic happens.

That's how you go from thinking about YOU as being just one person, to YOU being one person who is part of a group.

This book is my attempt to collect and share loads of lessons that I have learned from working with other people. Picking up their advice and guidance about how to work in a team, then combining it all to make something that's helpful for you and your team. Because when you discover how powerful you can be working in a team, you will realise that you can do amazing things and make a real difference in this world.

SO LET'S FIND OUT ALL THE WAYS IN WHICH YOU CAN DO IT.

ANYTHING YOU PUT YOUR MIND TO.

TOGETHER.

LET'S TURN THE PAGE AND GET STARTED.

M.R.

BE KIND TO YOURSELF

1

I WANT TO START THIS BOOK BY TALKING ABOUT
SOMETHING I'M NOT VERY GOOD AT.

TAKING BREAKS.

Let me explain — late in 2020, I hurt my shoulder, badly, which made it hard for me to run without feeling pain in my arms. Then, early in 2021, I hurt my ankle too.

It was a really difficult time for me. My body was in a lot of pain, but I was trying my hardest to ignore it and carry on playing games for Manchester United and England. The harder I tried to keep going, the harder it became to do anything. I couldn't run as fast as I used to, and I wasn't as strong as I was the year before.

BUT THERE WERE A LOT OF IMPORTANT GAMES HAPPENING AT THE END OF THE SEASON, AND I WANTED TO HELP MY TEAM AS BEST I COULD. SO I KEPT GOING, EVEN THOUGH I WAS HURTING, AS I THOUGHT THAT WAS THE BEST THING FOR ME TO DO.

2

I finished the football season with Manchester United in May, but we lost the Europa League Final in a penalty shootout.

I HAD PLAYED IN
59 GAMES

(WHICH IS A LOT OF GAMES!)

AND WHILE I SCORED 21 GOALS, I DON'T THINK IT WAS MY BEST SEASON EVER.

When I get to the end of a season I usually reflect on the things that went well and those that didn't, and I spent a little bit of time wondering what might have happened if my body wasn't hurting so much. Maybe, if I had taken a break when I first started noticing pain in my shoulder, I could have solved the problem quickly, rather than pushing myself to keep playing. Looking back, I still don't know if I made the right decision –

ALL I KNOW IS
I TRIED MY BEST.

Then, in June and July of 2021, I was at the UEFA European Championships with England. My shoulder still wasn't 100%, so I didn't play as much of the championships as I would have liked, but it was amazing to be part of the team – *AND THAT SUMMER THE ENGLAND TEAM WERE INCREDIBLE.*

TO ANYONE WHO WATCHED AND SUPPORTED ENGLAND OVER THE UEFA EURO 2020, I WANT TO **THANK YOU** FROM THE BOTTOM OF MY HEART.

We lost in the Final to Italy on penalties, but that was an incredible summer, and I'll cherish those memories for the rest of my life.

Now, I don't like talking about that Final much, but I want to explain
a little bit about what happened.

That day of the Final – England vs Italy – felt like it was going to be a
special day for football fans all over the country. It had been 55 years
since England had been in the final of an international tournament –
1966, when England won the World Cup. And just like in 1966, the Final
of UEFA EURO 2020 was played at Wembley Stadium in London. The
atmosphere was beyond belief.

It's hard to put into words my emotions before that game. Everyone in
the England camp knew that Italy would be a hard opponent, but we all
felt that if we gave it our best, *IF WE ALL PLAYED AT 100%,
WE MIGHT BE ABLE TO DO SOMETHING AMAZING.*

I was watching from the bench for nearly all of the game. It was so tense.
When my friend Luke Shaw scored early I thought Wembley was going to
erupt in sheer joy. The noise was like nothing I'd ever heard before! There
were over 60,000 people in Wembley that day, most of them supporting
England, and it really made me think that we were going to do it. That we
were going to pull it off and win UEFA EURO 2020 . . .

But, unfortunately for us, Italy were just too good that day. They didn't panic, they kept winning the ball back and they controlled the pace of the game, until they eventually scored a goal, making the score 1–1. It was hard to watch, and the match went to extra time. And in the last moments of the game, just before the penalty shootout, the England manager, Gareth Southgate, put me on.

I was nominated to take the third penalty for England against Italy. At the time I stepped up to take my shot, Italy had scored two of their three attempts, while England had scored their first two. My kick would have taken England 3–2 up in the shootout and given us a big advantage for the remaining penalties.

Now, I don't normally get nervous when playing football. But that day, when I picked up the ball to take my penalty, *I FELT DIFFERENT, AS IF SOMETHING WAS OFF.* Maybe it was the emotion of the game. Maybe it was seeing how big the Italian goalkeeper – Gianluigi Donnarumma – looked in that goal. Maybe my shoulder was playing on my mind a bit too much. For some reason, my brain wasn't telling me 'Just try your best', like it normally did. Instead, it was saying

'YOU HAVE TO BE **PERFECT**'.

I tried a different penalty style from the ones I normally do. I did a stuttering run up, where I paused a little bit on my way to kick the ball, trying to get Donnarumma to move early and make the penalty easier. By the time I got to the ball to take my shot, Donnarumma had dived the wrong way . . . but my shot missed the goal by an inch, hitting the post and going wide.

It was the biggest game of my England career. The biggest game for the England team and England fans in 55 years. And in one of the most important moments I missed a chance to give us a lead. In the end, England lost that Final 3–2 to Italy.

After the game, I was overcome by emotions. *I WAS ANGRY. I WAS SAD. I FELT LIKE A FAILURE. I FELT LIKE I HAD LET EVERYONE – INCLUDING PEOPLE LIKE YOU, HOLDING THIS BOOK – DOWN. AND THINGS GOT EVEN WORSE THE DAY AFTER THE FINAL.* I woke up to horrible messages from people all over the country who were frustrated and angry at everyone who had missed a penalty for England. A lot of the things that were said were horrible and racist – bringing up my skin colour and my background, and saying that was why I had let my country down. Some said that I should be kicked out of the country. Or that I missed on purpose because I am a Black man and I don't care about England. There is a painting of my face in my hometown in Manchester, and someone was so angry that I didn't score my penalty that they vandalised it. Seeing all that happen, I was numb. I even struggled to get out of bed for a few days.

LET ME TELL YOU, I LOVE ENGLAND, AND PLAYING FOR MY COUNTRY IS ONE OF THE GREATEST HONOURS I HAVE HAD AS A FOOTBALLER. I CAN ACCEPT CRITICISM IF I'VE HAD A BAD GAME, BUT SOME OF THE COMMENTS MY TEAMMATES AND I RECEIVED AFTER THAT FINAL CROSSED A LINE, LEADING TO ONE OF THE HARDEST WEEKS OF MY LIFE.

Thankfully, in the days that followed, something amazing happened. Something that helped get me through. People from all over the country – people like you – travelled to the painting and left messages of support for me and my teammates. People reached out to the England team to say 'Thank you for reaching the Final', to tell us that they were proud of everything we had done. I got letters telling me to ignore the racist things people said, and instead to think about the good things that had happened during the competition. I can't describe what that meant to me.

It was a long season for Manchester United and England, and both my teams lost in the Final on penalties – and coming that close to winning a trophy, only to miss out twice, hurt even more. But those messages of support, the kindness that those people showed me, helped remind me of the kindness I needed to show myself to get better.

Even though I was tired from the season I wanted to get right back to it, to find a way to go back to being 100% in everything I do. But after talking with my friends, family, coaches at Manchester United and some doctors, I realised that trying to work through all the pain, both physically and mentally, wasn't the best way for me to look after myself, or the people around me. I wanted to get back to being 100% when I was playing football, but to do that I had to have some time being 100% Marcus. Just regular Marcus, who eats a bit too much sugar and loves wearing a tracksuit at home.

WE WILL NEVER LET THE HATERS WIN

YOU ARE …
BEAUTIFUL
BRAVE
BLESSED
LOVED

YOU ARE A CHAMPION IN OUR EYES

IN THE END, I MADE A DECISION TO GET SOME HELP AND TO TAKE A BREAK. It wasn't an easy decision – I knew that I would end up missing a lot of games for Manchester United by doing so. And late on in the summer of 2021 I went to the hospital to have surgery on my shoulder, and I wasn't able to play football for three whole months.

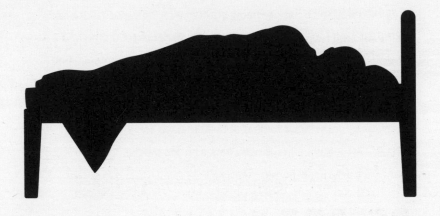

It took a little bit of time for me to get used to it. My arm was in a sling for a few days and I couldn't exercise or do all the things I normally do in my daily routine as a footballer. I'll admit I wasn't in the best of moods during that time. I didn't want to leave my bedroom or see my friends. I watched Manchester United start their new season from home, but, to be honest, that made me feel a little lost.

I FELT PRETTY DOWN FOR ABOUT FIVE DAYS AFTER THE SURGERY, BUT THEN I WAS ABLE TO START OPENING UP TO PEOPLE AROUND ME. My brothers were a big help at the time. Even though I was doing everything the doctors told me to, I wanted everything to sort itself out quicker so I could go back to playing football. When I got frustrated Dwaine and Dane would step in and remind me to go easy on myself, and that my shoulder wouldn't be damaged forever. They would tell me to listen to my body and not to overdo things if I felt a little bit of pain, no matter how much I wanted to get back to how I used to be. They would check in on me and ask how I was doing every day, which in turn helped me to remember to look after myself.

There's this phrase,

'YOU HAVE TO WALK BEFORE YOU CAN RUN',

that is all about making sure you do things in the right order and at the right speed. I thought about that a lot when I was recovering. Slowly, I realised that the best thing I could do was to look after myself properly, so that when I did play again, I'd be the best possible version I could be.

Have you ever been watching television and the remote control stopped working? What's the first thing you normally do? Press down even **harder** on the buttons, right? Then you probably try holding the remote at all sorts of different angles, hoping that the signal gets picked up. Then, if the remote is still not working, I bet you tried putting in new batteries. Or maybe you took the batteries out of something else you have, and put them in the remote.

Your body and brain can be a bit like the remote control when it's not sending the signals it usually does, because your batteries have run out. But rather than press down harder, or put yourself at difficult angles . . .

THE BEST THING YOU CAN DO IS **STOP FOR A BIT** AND GET YOURSELF A FRESH PAIR OF BATTERIES.

IT CAN BE HARD TO DO WHEN THINGS ARE BUSY, OR WHEN YOU WANT TO REACH A GOAL QUICKLY, BUT SOMETIMES GOING AT A PACE YOU'RE COMFORTABLE WITH IS BETTER THAN GOING AS FAST AS POSSIBLE.

13

And if you're wondering what the best way is to recharge your batteries . . . well, that's something I'm still learning. There are some things I can recommend to you that have been really useful to me over the years, *LIKE MAKING SURE YOU GET A GOOD NIGHT'S SLEEP.* When I was a kid I never wanted to go to bed on time as I had all this energy, but now I'm older I realise how important it is to rest, so you can be fresh for the adventures ahead of you. I have my own little routine where I try to go to my room at the same time every night and listen to something that calms me down before I drift off. My friends say I sleep like a cat because of the way I wander home after a long day and fall asleep quickly, but I spent a lot of time making sure my bedroom is as comfortable as possible.

EXERCISE IS IMPORTANT TOO, AND I'M NOT JUST TALKING ABOUT RUNNING AROUND PLAYING FOOTBALL (ALTHOUGH THAT HELPS ME!).

EXERCISE SHOULD BE ENJOYABLE AND SOMETHING YOU FEEL CALM AFTER DOING

(YES, EVEN IF YOU LOSE).

If you're the type of person who dreads going to PE lessons then don't worry, exercise can be as simple as going for a walk when you can, taking in all the sights and sounds of a day. If you walk to and from your school every day, you're already doing exercise, and if you don't walk to school every day, don't worry. Take some time to look at what sort of exercise might interest you. There are loads of different ways to get your body moving, be it team sports or something you can practise at home by yourself. The key thing is doing something active, even for just a little bit.

Another great way to look after yourself is to look to the people around you for advice and guidance. In my life, I've always tried to have positive people around me, who can lend me a helping hand when I feel low or start to think negatively. When you're ill or have suffered a setback it can be easy to think that you'll be that way forever. That maybe the bad thing that has happened will be a bad thing that will keep happening for the rest of your life. It's times like this when turning to your friends, family and other people you trust can be so important.

WHEN YOU SURROUND YOURSELF AND OPEN UP TO PEOPLE WHO CAN BE KIND TO YOU, **YOU LEARN HOW TO BE KIND TO YOURSELF,** AND WHEN YOU LEARN HOW TO BE KIND TO YOURSELF, **YOU CAN THEN LEARN TO BE KIND TO OTHERS IN TURN.**

(AND THERE'LL BE MORE OF THIS IN THE NEXT CHAPTER!)

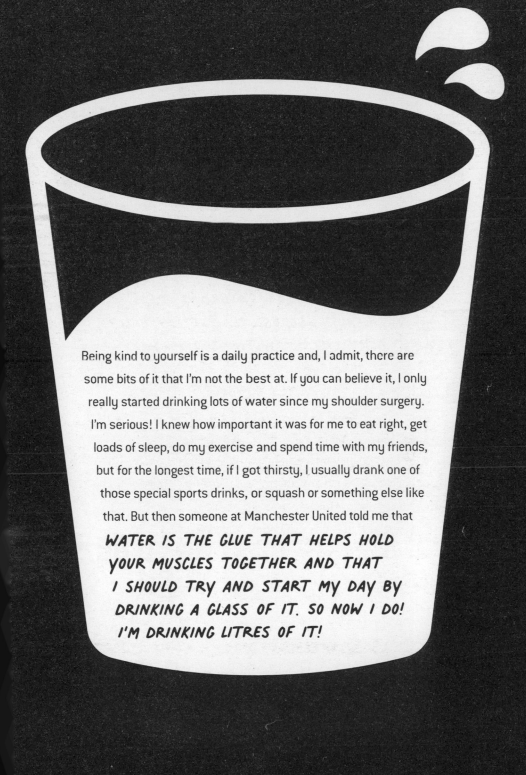

Being kind to yourself is a daily practice and, I admit, there are some bits of it that I'm not the best at. If you can believe it, I only really started drinking lots of water since my shoulder surgery. I'm serious! I knew how important it was for me to eat right, get loads of sleep, do my exercise and spend time with my friends, but for the longest time, if I got thirsty, I usually drank one of those special sports drinks, or squash or something else like that. But then someone at Manchester United told me that

WATER IS THE GLUE THAT HELPS HOLD YOUR MUSCLES TOGETHER AND THAT I SHOULD TRY AND START MY DAY BY DRINKING A GLASS OF IT. SO NOW I DO! I'M DRINKING LITRES OF IT!

It sounds simple, but looking after yourself is making sure you make time for the little things so that you are fit, fresh and firing for the big things down the line. Your 100% will look a little bit different every single day, so don't feel guilty about days where you didn't get as much done as you'd have liked.

Try to think about the things you like doing most in life.

ON A PERFECT SATURDAY ARE YOU READING BOOKS? PLAYING FOOTBALL? GOING OUTSIDE WITH YOUR MATES? OR MAYBE AT HOME ON YOUR GAMES CONSOLE.

Whatever it is, try and find a way to do that, just for a little bit. Try to look at your hobbies as much as possible and then find ways you can build on them. If you're really into music, maybe one day you can try and find someone new to listen to. If you're someone who likes cooking, why not have a go at one of your favourite recipes next time? Like doing puzzles? Why don't you see if crosswords are for you?

IT'S PARTICULARLY IMPORTANT TO REMEMBER TO BE KIND TO YOURSELF WHEN THINGS AREN'T GOING WELL.

I know that when I lose a game of football, all these little things I do stop me from feeling too low. It's important to keep a balance in your life, and not to be too hard on yourself when things don't go right.

I hope that you think of reading this book as a way to rest and relax, rather than something you have to do. We're going to spend a lot of time talking about chasing your dreams and how you have the power to help change the world, but it's going to be harder for you to do that if you feel tired and stressed out all the time. I want you to make sure you always have fresh mental batteries for whatever adventures you have ahead.

Before we get into anything in this book, I want you to know how important it is for you to look after yourself. Learning how to be kind to yourself can be just as important as being kind to others, and is the first step in learning how to change the world.

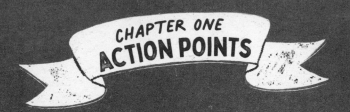

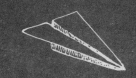

1. NO ONE'S PERFECT JUST HUMAN!

There is a belief that in order for a person to be worthy of attention and applause, we have to be perfect at everything we do, all of the time. This belief is called

PERFECTIONISM.

A LOT OF PEOPLE TRY TO BE PERFECT. BUT TRUST ME — NO ONE, AND I MEAN <u>NO ONE</u>, IS PERFECT!

Here are a few facts I try to carry with me every single day:

- We all make mistakes. If we didn't make mistakes, we wouldn't have the opportunity to learn what to do differently next time.

- Our bodies and minds all have limits — that's normal. (Otherwise, we'd be robots!)

Just like nature has different seasons, so do humans. We need time and space to grow, the right conditions and environment to sprout and blossom, and we all bloom at different times. (We all need to hibernate too! Sleep and rest are just as important as work and play.)

Have there been times where you've felt the need to be perfect at any cost? Have you ever had a moment where you've been told by someone that you have to be

10/10? **A+?**

NUMBER ONE?

COMPLETELY PERFECT?

Write down three reasons why you're proud of yourself. It could be something you've done well, or times you've made a positive difference in someone's life.

Think about this list the next time you find yourself comparing yourself to others, or upset that you made a mistake. The more you remind yourself of what you uniquely bring to this world, the easier it will be to accept that you're a human with flaws . . . just like every other human on the planet.

2. RACISM IS NEVER OKAY: SOME RIGHTS AND RESPONSIBILITIES

I strongly believe that if we want to make the world a better place then we all have to work together to make a world that no longer has racism, sexism, homophobia or any other form of discrimination. One way we can tackle racism is to understand that we all have various rights and responsibilities – to our friends, to our family and to everyone around us.

If you're the target of racism, you have the **RIGHT** to:

- **Refuse to laugh at racist 'jokes'.**
- **Feel pride in your heritage and community.**
- **Be treated equally in every situation and never be put down based on who you are.**

If you're not the target of racism, you have the **RESPONSIBILITY** to:

- Listen to your friends about their experiences with racism and take what they say seriously.

- Speak up to your family, friends and others when they say or do something racist.

- Think through the ways you're treated differently in society just for being born white.

- Learn more about the experiences and achievements of people of colour in Britain and their long history of fighting for equality.

CAN YOU THINK OF OTHER RIGHTS AND RESPONSIBILITIES TO ADD TO THIS LIST?

3. TAKING CARE OF YOURSELF HELPS OUT EVERYONE

Remember I talked about how important it is to recharge your batteries and get some rest instead of continuing to push yourself for other people? We all want to help out our community and be there for the people we care about, whether it's helping our team win a football match, working together at school on a group project to get a good grade, or being there for our family members. But as I found out in my own life, we can't be the best version of ourselves if we're tired, cranky, hungry, sad, stressed out or healing from an injury!

When you take the time to care for yourself — getting enough sleep, talking to a trusted adult about your problems, doing things you like to do in your free time — you'll feel more energised, and capable of using your energy to help the other people in your life. Remember you deserve to give yourself just as much attention and love as others!

Make a list of some ways you can take care of yourself.

- What are your favourite things to do to relax?
- Who are your favourite people to talk to?
- What is your favourite music to listen to, and TV shows to watch?
- What are your favourite ways to move your body?
- What makes you laugh?

MAKE SURE YOU TAKE THE TIME TO DO ALL OF THE THINGS ON YOUR LIST REGULARLY. THEY WILL BECOME YOUR GO-TO WAYS OF CARING FOR YOURSELF AND REMINDING YOURSELF HOW MUCH YOU MATTER.

BE KIND TO OTHERS

2

DOWN BY THE AREA I GREW UP, THERE WAS A SHOP RUN BY A GUY CALLED GREG.

Greg opened his shop when I was about seven or eight years old. On top of being this nice, friendly shopkeeper, Greg is the most amazing chef. His shop looks like a regular corner shop, but at the front there's always one or two bits of hot food that Greg sells throughout the day. The first time my family and I went in the shop, before we could even ask for what we wanted or tell him who we were, Greg gave us a whole load of food that he thought we'd like. He gave us dumplings, patties and this amazing curried goat stew he'd made.

If you've never tried Caribbean food before, you are missing out. The flavours are on another level! But you have to watch out for the spice, too. Greg's curried goat is some of the best I've ever had, but he puts a lot of this chilli pepper called 'Scotch bonnet' in it. It was so hot it made me sweat the first time I tried it! I thought I was going to start breathing fire!

The shop is near a little green where a few of my mates and I used to play football after school. Greg knew our family well, and he knew that my mum would often leave for work early in the mornings and that sometimes she would be working late, until 10 o'clock at night. My family didn't have the most money when we were growing up, so my mum often worked three jobs in one day just to keep the lights and heating on.

Every now and then, after school, I'd go into Greg's shop to get some sweets. But whenever I tried to pay for them Greg would always shake his head. The first time it happened I thought he was going to give me a telling off about buying sugar when my mum wasn't around, but that didn't happen. Instead, Greg would always tell me to keep my money.

'You can have the sweets, but keep the money,' he'd tell me. 'I'll talk to your mum when she next comes into the shop.'

Sometimes I would play football on the green outside my house all day, until it got dark, and then when I was tired and hungry I'd go into Greg's, looking to buy some sweets or some biscuits. But, just like the first time, Greg refused to take my money.

Sometimes I thought he was giving me food that was about to go off, or that he just wanted me out of his shop before I could make too much of a mess — most evenings I'd be carrying a football and wearing muddy football boots — but whenever I tried to pay Greg, he'd shake his head and tell me not to worry.

It was his little way of looking after me, because he knew we didn't always have a lot of food at home, and he wanted to do something nice for my mum and me.

GREG HAD BEEN KIND TO ME, JUST BECAUSE HE COULD. AND WHAT HE DID MADE ME REALISE THAT

CHOOSING TO BE KIND TO OTHERS IS ONE OF THE MOST IMPORTANT THINGS YOU CAN DO IN LIFE.

I know there are a lot of sayings out there like 'kindness is weakness' or 'nice guys finish last', and as you grow up you might hear a lot of talk about how it's much more important that you look after 'number one' – yourself – instead of helping others. But I don't think it's a case of one or the other. I think it's important that you look after yourself, of course, but in my mind that just makes you more capable of helping others. I also think that living in a world where everyone's helping each other makes it easier for people to look after themselves when they need to.

WHEN YOU ARE KIND TO SOMEONE ELSE, IT CAN START OFF THIS CHAIN REACTION WHERE THE PERSON YOU WERE KIND TO IS THEN KIND TO SOMEONE ELSE, AND THEN THAT PERSON IS KIND TO SOMEONE ELSE, UNTIL LOADS OF PEOPLE START THINKING ABOUT HOW THEY CAN BE KIND TO OTHER PEOPLE.

Some of you might remember the anti-food-poverty project I helped set up in 2020. I honestly don't think I would have been able to do that if it wasn't for the kindness that was shown to me by people like Greg when I was growing up. For years, Greg fed me, no questions asked, because he thought it was important I had something nice to eat after I played football. He did that for children all across Button Lane, and that kindness meant our parents and other adults in the area had one less thing to worry about. Which meant they were able to give their attention to other important things, like cleaning up the parks or making sure the roads were safe when the kids go to school.

Greg's kindness was just one instance in my life where I met a person who just wanted to help others, no questions asked. And let me tell you now, those people, people like Greg, are some of the best you can surround yourself with. They're the sort of person I try my hardest to be like. What he did for my mum and me enabled me to ask people around the country to be kind and support the campaign in 2020, which in turn led to millions of children across the UK getting the food they desperately needed.

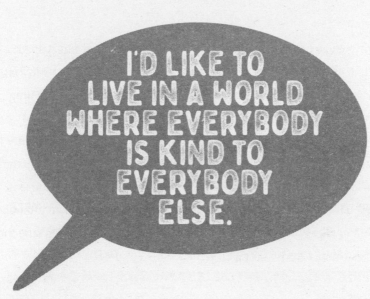

I'D LIKE TO
LIVE IN A WORLD
WHERE EVERYBODY
IS KIND TO
EVERYBODY
ELSE.

IT DOESN'T MATTER WHO IT IS. IT COULD BE YOUR
MUM, A SIBLING, A TEACHER, YOUR BEST FRIEND
OR JUST SOMEONE YOU'VE BUMPED INTO. BUT IF
SOMEONE IS ASKING FOR HELP, OR IF IT LOOKS LIKE
THEY NEED HELP, YOU SHOULD TRY YOUR BEST
TO HELP THEM.

I still get help from people who have less money or aren't as fortunate
as I am now, and I try my best, every single day, to be kind and help
other people in return. Trust me, no matter how many goals I score,
I'm never going to be the best at reading maps, so I really appreciate
it when someone can help me with directions when I am lost. On the
flip side, I know that when I play football there are ways I can help my

team outside of scoring or creating goals: I might need to talk to my teammates so they can see things better, or maybe track back and help on defence. Sometimes when a new footballer comes to Manchester United they might need my help showing them around, or even finding them a hairdresser! There are so many different ways you can help the people around you, and the smallest thing can go a long way.

AND DON'T EVER THINK THAT YOU WON'T BE ABLE TO HELP SOMEONE BECAUSE YOU'RE NOT THE RIGHT PERSON. EVERYBODY IS DIFFERENT, AND DIFFERENT PEOPLE HAVE DIFFERENT STRENGTHS, WHICH MEANS THAT DIFFERENT PEOPLE CAN HELP WITH DIFFERENT THINGS. NO MATTER WHAT THE PROBLEM IS, SOMEONE OUT THERE WILL BE ABLE TO HELP.

AND SOMETIMES THAT SOMEONE IS GOING TO BE YOU!

Try not to get put off by the idea of being kind to someone if they are different from you, or someone who you don't know, and don't think you should only be kind to people who have been kind to you first. The way I see it, showing kindness leads to more kindness – from you, to the person you've helped, and then to the people around both of you.

I'll admit that when I got involved with the anti-food-poverty project a lot of people asked me if it was a good decision. If it was really something I should be doing. There are some people who want footballers to just 'focus on their football' and never talk about anything else. But it didn't matter to me what anybody thought. When I was a kid I relied on the help of the people around me, so when I saw children during the pandemic who needed help, I knew I was the right person to step up.

IF YOU'RE THINKING ABOUT BEING KIND AND HELPING ANOTHER PERSON, DON'T BE PUT OFF BY WHAT SOMEONE ELSE THINKS. DON'T PAY ANY ATTENTION TO WHAT SOMEONE ELSE MIGHT SAY. THAT'S NOT WHAT'S IMPORTANT. WHAT'S IMPORTANT IS THAT SOMEONE IS STRUGGLING, AND THEY MAY NOT WANT THE ENTIRE WORLD TO KNOW, BUT IF YOU CAN SEE IT, IT MIGHT BE WORTH YOU REACHING OUT.

SOMETIMES I FIND IT
DIFFICULT
TO ASK FOR HELP.

I think that happens to everyone from time to time. It's not that you don't want help, or that asking for help is a bad thing, but more that you don't want other people to know you might be having a tough time. I have friends who'd much rather get lost for 10 minutes than stop and ask someone for directions. When I was really young there were times when I needed help with my shoelaces, or tying a tie with my shirt, but I was too nervous to ask for help because I didn't want people to laugh at me.

Something I've realised as I've got older is that there is no shame in asking for help. Helpful people like helping others, so you don't need to worry if someone is rude to you for not knowing something – that says more about them than it does about you. I always want someone to offer me help before I get really stuck, and I try my best to help other people when I can see they need it too.

But equally, if you can't help, then don't feel bad. Sometimes I'll try to help my mum or one of my siblings and they'll tell me, 'It's alright, I'm good now. I figured it out,' and I'll carry on with my day.

Try not to get worried if someone turns down your offer of help. The way I see it, the person who would prefer to do it themselves will learn how to take care of their task, so you get more time to help someone else later down the line. But don't take one person turning down your help as a reason for not offering it to someone else the next day.

AND DON'T BE FRIGHTENED BY THE IDEA OF HELPING SOMEONE. YOU DON'T HAVE TO CLOSE THIS BOOK RIGHT NOW AND TRY TO FIGURE OUT A SOLUTION TO CLIMATE CHANGE OR ANYTHING LIKE THAT. BUT I THINK IN YOUR AVERAGE DAY THERE IS ALWAYS AN OPPORTUNITY OR TWO TO BE KIND TO SOMEONE ELSE. YOU PROBABLY ALREADY GIVE A LITTLE KINDNESS IN YOUR LIFE EVERY DAY WITHOUT EVEN THINKING ABOUT IT.

HAVE YOU HELD A DOOR OPEN FOR SOMEONE TODAY?

YOU'VE HELPED THEM.

HAVE YOU SAID 'BLESS YOU' WHEN SOMEONE SNEEZED?

THEN YOU'VE LET SOMEONE KNOW THAT YOU'RE THINKING ABOUT THEM.

DID YOU HELP ONE OF YOUR CLASSMATES AT SCHOOL WHEN THEY WERE STUCK WITH SOME CLASSWORK?

THAT COUNTS AS KINDNESS.

Have you ever helped someone pick up something they've dropped? Or hugged a family member when they seemed down? What about reminding a friend about something they need to do later in the day? What about the moment when you're on a bus or a train and an elderly person or a pregnant person steps on, and someone tries to offer them their seat?

All these gestures count as kindness, and when as many people as possible do all of these little things, they add up to create something great. A community of people who are constantly looking after each other.

There have been times where I've lost a football game but I've still tried my best to be polite and kind to football fans who would like to take a selfie with me, or who ask for my shirt. Why? Because I think kindness is a way you can open up doors in people's lives. My mum brought me up with the words:

'TREAT EVERYONE HOW YOU WOULD WANT TO BE TREATED',

and it's something I've always carried with me.

Throughout my life I've had to be kind to people who haven't been the nicest to me or my family. There have been times when I've gone to help someone and they've unfortunately tried to take advantage of that. This might happen to you one day, or it might have already happened to you, or someone you love. If it does happen, I want to tell you that I am sorry, but I hope it doesn't put you off being kind in future. It's sad to say but there are some people in the world who believe being kind makes you 'soft' and that being unkind is the only way to be 'strong enough' to be successful in life.

I DON'T BELIEVE THAT.

If you've ever shown kindness to someone and they've turned around and been unkind back, try your best to keep your head up. Just know in your heart that when you choose to be kind, you're choosing to be the right thing, and if you decide to be kind to someone who has been mean to you before, you might change their perspective on what's important in life. Taking time out of your day to be kind is something to be applauded, even if you don't always get a 'thank you' back.

Take it from me — I grew up watching my mum struggle with a busy house and not that much money, and she managed to find time to be kind and help others. In the area I grew up in there were people like Greg who often went out of their way to be kind, because they understood that that's the way small communities survive: with everyone pitching in, sharing what they can, and making a little last a long time.

In fact, I've got one more story about Greg for you. Now that I'm an adult and I know everything he's done for me, I try my best to help him out whenever I go back to Button Lane . . . but he never lets me! When I try to pay him back for all the food he gave me, he tells me not to worry. We argue about it for a while but he always tells me that he's ok, and that he wants me to focus on being kind to other people who really need my help.

(He always wins the arguments, but whenever he's not looking I sneak some money into a friend's pocket and tell them to take him out for dinner. Sorry, Greg!)

That's the power of kindness. When you help one person you give them the power to help someone else. Which gives the next person the power to help someone else. Over time, this chain gets bigger and bigger, and you can go from helping one person to helping your local area, to maybe even someday helping the country or even the entire world! Never underestimate your actions – even the smallest act of kindness can have the biggest impact.

KINDNESS

IS A CHOICE,

SO CHOOSE TO
BE KIND
AS MUCH AS POSSIBLE.

IT IS ONE OF THE MOST IMPORTANT THINGS A PERSON CAN EVER DO.

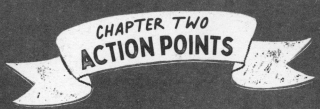

1. WE BECOME STRONGER WHEN WE'RE THERE FOR EACH OTHER

We all want to be part of a community where we feel like we matter, where we feel we're safe and cared for. And the good news is that we have the power to create that type of society through kindness. When we make the effort to practise kindness toward others, we build relationships and bonds that can last a lifetime. We show up for each other. We make a difference in each other's lives. We remind each other that none of us have to walk alone.

Think about the National Health Service. Most people who earn money in the UK help to pay for the NHS and keep it running, so that everyone – no matter who you are, no matter whether you can afford it or not – has free health care. A big reason the NHS exists, and has so much support, is thanks to kindness. We agree that we all deserve to be healthy and live our best lives. We all deserve to be able to visit the doctor and take medicine. We all deserve to make the most of the lives that we're given. We don't need to prove why someone should care about us or help us heal from being sick. We know it's the right thing to do.

Think about your school and your community. Are there ways they could be even kinder towards the people, animals, wildlife and spaces in it?

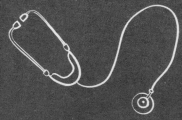

Write down three acts of kindness that could make life better where you live. For example, could people clear up after themselves a little better? Could people be kinder to shop workers in your area?

2. IT'S A TEAM EFFORT – HOW CAN YOU HELP?

Everyone has the power to practise kindness. Every person has talents that are unique to them. Every person also has the opportunity to use their unique talents to help the people around them.

What are you good at? What do you know that could help someone else? How can you show someone you care?

Do you like baking biscuits or cakes? Do you have fun creating cards or other art? Do you like helping your friends talk about how they're feeling and giving them advice? Write down five things you enjoy doing. Then next to each of those five things, write a way you can practise kindness for others through that activity. How does what you're doing help other people?

THINGS I ENJOY DOING.	I CAN BE KIND BY...
1.	1.
2.	2.
3.	3.
4.	4.
5.	5.

3. KINDNESS IS FOR EVERYONE (INCLUDING YOU!)

We've talked a lot about how everyone deserves kindness, not just your family and friends or people who look and act like you. All living beings on this planet have the right to be treated with kindness, dignity and respect. So many of the world's problems — from racism, sexism, homophobia, and beyond — could be fixed if we remembered this seemingly simple fact!

It's also true that people can take advantage of your kindness. They can expect you to be there for them but not act as kindly towards you in return. Or they might be downright mean to you, deciding that you don't deserve their kindness because of how you look or talk, what your skin colour is, where you're from, what religion you practise, how much money your family has, because you're LGBTQ+, or any number of reasons that aren't your fault. Many times when people act unkindly, it's because they're carrying a lot of hate, fear and sadness around. It can be really unfortunate, and sometimes it brings about a cycle of anger and hatred in one person leading to more anger and hatred in others.

There's a saying: **'Hurt people hurt people'.** It means that some people who have been hurt go on to hurt others around them. And here's something really important to remember: **you absolutely don't have to go out of your way to be kind to people who make you feel unsafe.** You deserve to be kind to yourself, too, which means protecting yourself from harm. There is room in this world to practise kindness towards others and also keep yourself safe.

I want you to write down three reasons why you deserve kindness. They can be as simple as **'I try my best'** or **'I like making people happy'.** Write those reasons down and put them somewhere you'll see them every day, like on a mirror or next to your bed, to remind yourself why you're just as worthy of receiving the same kindness that you put out into the world!

NO SUCH THING AS ((NORMAL))

3

Back at school, I had a friend called Jahedi. He was a really good cricketer.

(IF YOU'VE READ MY LAST BOOK, YOU'LL KNOW HOW COMPETITIVE I AM, SO I HOPE YOU UNDERSTAND THAT WHAT I'M ABOUT TO SAY IS A REALLY BIG DEAL.)

JAHEDI WAS A BETTER CRICKETER THAN ME.

He had this love for the game that really shone through whenever we played. He'd put a little bit of spin on the ball when he was bowling and he had this special ability to know where the batsman was likely to try to hit it in response. When we played together he'd always give orders to other fielders: where they should stand and who should be ready — telling us what was likely to happen next. Playing cricket with Jahedi, you'd think he had a crystal ball and he could see the future.

Jahedi and I became friends because we both loved playing sports, and I'd spend loads of PE lessons asking him how he was so much better than everyone else at cricket. Not in a jealous way or anything, but I was really curious to know what he was thinking when he played the game.

WHAT WAS HE LOOKING FOR? HOW DID HE KNOW THE BEST WAY TO MOVE HIS BODY WHEN HE WAS BOWLING? HOW DID HE MAKE DECISIONS ABOUT WHAT TO DO NEXT?

It was all different from how I played cricket, and I thought that difference, the difference in the way he thought, was really cool.

This really came out when we were batters. When I went to bat during PE lessons, I typically just tried to hit the ball with as much power as possible. Jahedi, however, was a lot more graceful than that. He knew when to go for power, but also when to go for softer, more defensive strikes on the ball so he wouldn't get out. And trust me, it was next to impossible to bowl him out. He was amazing.

The cogs in his brain worked differently from mine, and that's what helped make him a better cricketer.

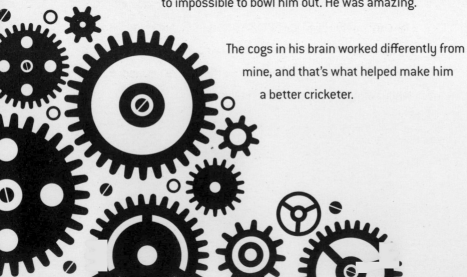

Talking about cricket with Jahedi was the first time I realised that even though someone didn't view something the same way I did, that didn't mean we couldn't get along, or that we couldn't enjoy the same things. It also opened my eyes to the idea that the way I saw the world might not be the smartest way, and there might be other, better ways to do things.

In my life I've been fortunate enough to live in some of the most multicultural areas of Manchester, surrounded by people from different cultures and different countries. I grew up in Wythenshawe, but I also spent time living in Moss Side, and I was originally born in a place called Withington. I've grown up living next to Black people who look like me, white people, Indian people, families from Eastern Europe – the works. Even though we all came from different parts of the world, we all found a way to connect with each other because we all had something in common – a love for our families and a real wish for our community to be better. We understood that we were better as a community when we worked together, and I'm forever grateful for the things I've learned and experienced while living side by side with them.

Now, with my football career, I work with people from all over the world. People from different races, different religions and different backgrounds and lifestyles from my own. Some of my teammates celebrate Christmas. Some fast for Ramadan. Some of us speak multiple languages and some of us don't eat meat.

It's taught me one really important thing about life:

THERE'S NO SUCH THING AS NORMAL.

THERE'S NO DEFAULT WAY FOR US ALL TO LIVE.

THERE'S NO ONE THING THAT WE ALL DO EXACTLY THE SAME.

WE'RE ALL A BIT DIFFERENT, AND THAT DIFFERENCE IS SOMETHING THAT SHOULD BE CELEBRATED.

(And there'll be more on this in the next chapter!)

There were times after school when Jahedi would invite me round to his house to watch television or do some homework. He was Muslim, and when we went to his house there were certain things that he politely asked me to do that initially seemed strange to me. But even though I wasn't used to doing some of these at first, I did as Jahedi asked as a show of respect to him and his family. For instance, I'd take off my shoes before I walked around his house (just like I did at my mum's!) and I would take special care to step through the front door with my right foot first. When Jahedi's parents greeted me, I would say 'Salam', and if I stayed over for dinner I would try to eat using my right hand, as they did. Jahedi explained to me that these things were known as 'Sunnah' — meaning they were traditions and practices of their prophet Muhammad.

My family is Christian, so we follow a different religion from Jahedi, but we too had some house rules. When my friends came to visit me at my home my mum would also ask them to take their shoes off before they walked around the house. Some people thought it was a little odd at first, but then my mum explained to them that she preferred it if people took their shoes off rather than risk bringing dirt over her clean carpets, and then they understood. And if someone ate dinner at my house my mum would often say a short prayer before we ate, as she thought it was important to bless the food and say thank you before our family meals. She wanted us to remember the hard work that had gone into bringing the food to our table.

I think we've all had moments where we've gone to someone else's house and been intrigued by how their world works. (I know every time I go to a different bathroom I have to figure out where they leave the towels or where they leave the soap!) But I find that everything clicks once someone explains to you how they've set up the space.

It's the same with life. We're all trying to do the same thing, we all just have different ways to do it. Often it takes someone communicating with you about how they like to do things to help you understand them better.

I think it's important that everyone's rights and way of life are respected wherever possible, no matter the colour of someone's skin, their religion, the way they dress, how they talk, or who they love. The way I see it, everybody starts life the same way: *YOU'RE BORN, YOU GROW UP, YOU MAKE FRIENDS, YOU EXPERIENCE THE WORLD AND YOU TRY TO FIGURE OUT WHAT YOU WANT TO DO WITH YOUR TIME.* You won't enjoy or understand everything in this world, but that doesn't mean you should think less of people who do enjoy things outside of the life you want to live. People who look different or act differently from you are just as worthy of the same rights, protections and happiness as you, and

YOU SHOULD ALWAYS TREAT EVERYONE WITH THE SAME LEVEL OF KINDNESS THAT YOU'D LIKE TO RECEIVE.

We're not all going to think in the same way, and I think that's brilliant because that means there's always more than one viewpoint and perspective on how to solve the big problems that affect us all. A good football team often has a mix of right-footed and left-footed players, as it opens up more passing angles on the pitch. The most successful businesses often have people from all different backgrounds as part of their leadership groups. This helps them to understand how to best serve all of their customers, who also come from a wide range of different backgrounds. I bet right now in your friendship circle you've got people with a whole mix of talents and skills, which means your group is never short of adventure and ideas.

EMBRACE THE DIFFERENCES THAT COME FROM LIFE.

As long as everyone is coming to situations from a respectful place, there is far more to be gained from working together than from cutting yourselves off from groups that seem different from you. This is not the easiest task, but loads of people joining forces to help the community go in one direction is better than lots of different groups pulling in loads of different directions at the same time.

When I was younger, every now and then my mum would do this routine if she felt I wasn't being a good team player — not doing my share of jobs around the house, or not being kind to my siblings, that kind of thing. She'd come up to me and say:

before pointing to her mouth.

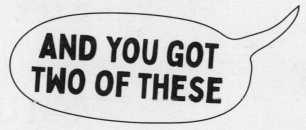

pointing to her ears.

That was her way of telling me to listen more than I talked. It's something I try to remember when I'm with someone who I want to understand better. If I want to learn more about people who have had different experiences from my own, I just need to listen more than I talk and make sure never to judge others because of where they come from or what they look like.

I also want to try my best to help others listen more. Not everyone is going to feel comfortable talking to bigger groups, so I need to do what I can to protect their voices whenever possible. If there was ever a time at school when one of my friends was picked on for their differences, I always tried to step in. Similarly, there were times at school when people tried to make fun of me because they knew I was on free school meals — that wasn't on, either, and that's when my friends stepped in and told any would-be bullies to leave me alone.

SOME PEOPLE ARE AFRAID OF WHAT THEY DON'T KNOW, AND THEY MIGHT NOT WANT THEIR VIEW OF THE WORLD TO BE CHALLENGED BY SOMETHING DIFFERENT. UNFORTUNATELY, THAT CAN LEAD THEM TO LASH OUT AND TRY TO GET RID OF THINGS THEY DON'T UNDERSTAND.

I see the same attitude as an adult. As a professional footballer in the men's game, I think it is my responsibility to help support the growth of the women's game too. If someone says, 'Girls playing football isn't normal', I always ask, 'Why not?', then try to start a conversation to explain why the women's game is just as amazing as the men's.

The difference between the two isn't quality, but opportunity. Did you know that between 1921 and 1971 women's football was banned in the United Kingdom? And you won't believe the reason why . . . because decision makers thought it was too popular and would distract fans away from the men's game! Women's football has always been brilliant, it's just that the people who were in charge of how the world of football worked tried to get rid of it, so it's now not considered to be as 'normal' as men's football. If you go through history you will find a lot of things are described as normal or traditional, but you'll also find that quite often this thinking has come from people who didn't necessarily want to include everyone.

THINK ABOUT HOW WOMEN'S FOOTBALL IS CALLED 'WOMEN'S FOOTBALL' AND MEN'S FOOTBALL IS JUST CALLED 'FOOTBALL'.

Think about who got to decide that men's football is the 'default'. I'm a Black man and all through my life the colour for 'normal' or 'neutral' plasters hasn't matched my skin tone. Does that mean my skin isn't normal? No! It means that at some point someone forgot to consider different skin tones before they decided one colour would be the 'default'.

Not everyone has the same advantages in life, and I think that's important to remember before you judge someone. The differences between us all can be scary at first — it is never easy when you encounter something you've never seen before — but it's important to push past any fear or confusion you may have and try to understand other people better so you can grow as a person. A lot of it can be as simple as how you voice things. There's a way you can ask 'What is that?' and come across as rude, and there's also a way you can say it that comes from a place of sincerity and wanting to know better. I always try to ask things in that way.

If you see someone doing something you don't understand, say something like, **'EXCUSE ME, BUT I'VE NEVER SEEN WHAT YOU'RE DOING BEFORE, CAN YOU TELL ME ABOUT IT?'**

Or, **'HEY, WHAT WAS THAT THING YOU JUST DID THERE? SHOULD I BE DOING THAT TOO?'**

Or maybe, **'IS THERE SOMETHING YOU'D LIKE ME TO KNOW BEFORE WE DO THIS THING TOGETHER?'**

Sometimes it can be as simple as,

IS THERE ANYTHING I CAN DO RIGHT NOW TO HELP MAKE YOUR LIFE EASIER?

As you go through life you may meet people who do things differently from you for reasons that you might not understand. Those times can be used as an opportunity for learning and understanding, rather than making fun of them. If someone eats their lunch differently from you at school, ask them why. Some people have different dietary needs or even some issues, which means that they need to avoid certain foods — or they might even ask you to avoid eating certain foods around them, so they don't get sick. I have a friend who is allergic to peanuts, so I'm always careful of what chocolate bars or other snacks I eat around them. A little change on my part can help them live their lives a lot easier!

And don't worry about asking questions if someone is doing something you've never seen before. Nobody knows everything about this world, and the best way to learn is to ask questions in a respectful and genuine manner and – really importantly – listen to the answers you get in return. You might not always get an answer from people, and sometimes what they say might not make sense, but that's ok.

THE IMPORTANT THING IS THAT YOU ASKED, AND THAT YOU'RE OPEN TO LEARNING. YOUR LIFE IS GOING TO BE FULL OF DISCOVERIES, AND IF YOU WANT TO KNOW SOMETHING YOU CAN EITHER BE BRAVE AND ASK SOMEONE OR TRY TO LEARN ABOUT IT BY READING UP ON THE SUBJECT.

Remember, too, that not everyone is going to want to do the same thing as everybody else. My main hobby at school was football, along with most of my friends, but that didn't mean we were better or cooler than people who had other interests. I know that at school there can be pressure to do what the group is doing and to not stick out too much, but never feel like you have to hide parts of yourself to fit in with a group or to feel 'normal'. If you have to do that, the group doesn't really understand you properly and you are better off somewhere else.

If you've read my first book, you'll know that I love a saying, and there's one I want to share with you now:

'GO WHERE YOU ARE NEEDED AND YOU ARE SEEN'.

It means that there will be times in life where, despite your best efforts, people will make you feel that you are not normal, and that they don't want you in their space. It can be really difficult trying to exist in an environment that doesn't make you feel like you belong, but always remember that there is somewhere in this world that is built with someone like you in mind. It may take you a little time to find it, but I promise it is out there. You might already have a space where you feel like you belong. For me, that space is my home, with my mum.

DON'T LET

ANYONE

PUT LIMITATIONS ON WHAT YOU CAN DO BECAUSE THEY DON'T AGREE WITH WHAT YOU'RE DOING, OR HOW YOU LOOK WHEN YOU DO IT.

I don't think it's right for people to have to pretend to enjoy something or pretend to be something they are not in order to better fit in with the 'cool crowd'. This isn't to say that people should only do what they love and not ever try to co-operate with other people, but I think if someone comes up to you and asks 'Why are you doing that?', you should be able to reply, 'Because it makes me happy', with pride. You only get one life, and it is YOUR life, so why waste time hiding yourself in case someone tries to call you 'embarrassing' or 'cringe'? Your smile is one of the most important and rare things in this world — don't let other people take it from you just because it makes them feel more comfortable.

And try your best not to take other people's smile away from them, either.

I TRY NOT TO THINK OF GROUPS AS 'US' AND 'THEM' BUT AS 'ALL OF US, TOGETHER, DOING OUR OWN THING'.

The differences between people should never be used as an excuse to build walls to separate ourselves from one another, but as an opportunity to build bridges between us. To learn from each other. To exchange ideas and grow. Together.

While we can all appear different at face value, it's important to remember that everyone has to eat, everyone has to drink and everyone needs somewhere to sleep. There is so much more in this world that connects us than separates us. I know it can be easy to think that we are all different people who are better off keeping ourselves to ourselves, but life and the world get so much better and so much more interesting when we reach out and connect with people from all walks of life. People who look different from us. People who love differently from us. People from different religions and people who have different perspectives on how to live. As long as people are respectful of each other and willing to collaborate, you should do what you can to reach out and learn from one another.

ONCE YOU'VE REALISED
THAT EVERYONE'S
THE SAME,
YOU REALISE
EVERYONE
IS WORTHY OF

LOVE AND RESPECT

1. FORGET ABOUT 'NORMAL'!

Everyone has had experiences where we've been made to feel like we're not 'normal', or have maybe thought that there's something wrong with us. It might be hard to believe, but this feeling has happened to all of us. That's right, even famous celebrities, successful athletes and businesspeople around the world! The most famous artists, musicians and writers of all time have had it too! It's part of being human.

EVERYONE HAS HAD A MOMENT WHERE THEY HAVE THOUGHT THEY WEREN'T NORMAL . . . WHICH MEANS THAT FEELING IS A TOTALLY NORMAL THING!

I want you to remember that all this really means is that there's variety among us, which is exciting and should be celebrated.

To help you throw out the old idea that you need to be 'normal', make a list of things that make you uniquely you. What makes you stand out from the crowd? What do you share with the people closest to you? What has made you feel 'weird'?

All these things are an important part of the story of YOU. This list could be anything, from having freckles, to sharing cultural traditions with your family, to liking a certain kind of music. Celebrate your uniqueness!

2. PUSH PAST THE FEAR OF DIFFERENCE

Can you think of a time you were scared of someone who was different from you? What about the situation felt scary? As you got to know more about the person or situation, how did you sense your feelings shifting?

Let's brainstorm. Find a piece of paper and write out the following words, filling in the gaps as you go!

- When I first met this person, I felt

  _____ and _____

- I was scared because

  _____

- As I grew to know them, I learned

  _____

- Learning more about this person made me feel

  _____ and _____

- If I met someone today who was scared like I was, my advice for them would be

  _____

CELEBRATE AND CHAMPION DIFFERENCE

4

WE'RE ABOUT HALFWAY THROUGH THIS BOOK NOW, SO I FEEL THAT THIS IS THE TIME TO SHARE SOMETHING A LITTLE DIFFERENT WITH YOU.

It used to be kind of a secret that only my close friends knew about, but I figure as you've come this far with me you should know it too.

Are you ready?

Here goes . . .

I REALLY LIKE THE NINJA TURTLES.

(No, seriously.)

Out of all the cartoons I used to watch on TV (and still watch now) the Ninja Turtles are my jam. Donatello, the purple one with the bō staff, was my favourite. I know most people prefer Michelangelo or Raphael, but Donatello was my guy. He was into science, inventing and tech, and I thought he was cool.

Why am I telling you all this? Well, when I was younger I used to do a LOT of Ninja Turtles drawings — at home, at school, during Breakfast Club. If I wasn't playing football you could probably find me drawing one of those green guys.

I changed primary schools at the end of Year 2, going from a school called Old Moat to Button Lane Primary for the start of Year 3. For that first month or so at Button Lane, when I didn't really know anyone or have many friends, I probably spent most early mornings and free play sessions in the classroom drawing. My teacher would help me cut out the Turtles and then I'd colour them in with crayons, customising them and making poster-sized prints. After I finished them I used to stick them up on my wall at home.

I loved making those Ninja Turtle posters, but if anyone in class walked past me when I was working on one I'd try my best to hide what I was doing.

Looking back, it's hard to say why I did that. I think it must have been because I was just starting out at a new school and I was shy — I didn't want anyone to think I was weird for being so obsessed with the Ninja Turtles.

BUT THE LONGER I SPENT DRAWING, THE MORE MY CLASSMATES WOULD ASK ME WHAT I WAS DOING.

At first, I was wary of opening up to them. I thought they would make fun of me for drawing Donatello so much, or that they would call my drawings rubbish. But the other kids genuinely wanted to know what I was doing. Drawing made me happy, and I guess some people just wanted to know what was bringing a smile to the new kid's face. I was nervous, but slowly I opened up and showed my classmates what I was doing, and while not everyone was into drawing, or as into the Ninja

Turtles as me (one kid told me that Leonardo – the leader of the Ninja Turtles – was cooler than Donatello!), I think a lot of my classmates respected how much time I spent on these drawings. A few of the friends I made even told me not to hide what I was doing, but to ask our teacher to put the posters on the wall in the classroom. That put a smile on my face.

What could have been a hobby that I stopped doing there and then ended up being a hobby I have carried on to this day. It made me realise that **just because I was doing something different from the crowd didn't mean I had to hide it from anyone.**

The friends I made at school liked me, and they wanted me to feel comfortable showing off all parts of my personality. Not just the things that were cool or 'normal' for a boy to do at school, like play football, but everything about me, including the things I did that were different.

It's something we should always try to do for the people around us. *TRY TO GIVE THEM SPACE SO THEY CAN FEEL OK ABOUT REVEALING ALL OF THEIR PERSONALITY, AND DON'T MAKE THEM FEEL LIKE THEY NEED TO HIDE PARTS OF WHO THEY ARE.* As you know from the previous chapter, everyone is different, and if we celebrate those differences we can create a world in which everyone feels a bit more comfortable.

That's why when you encounter someone's passion you should treat it with care and respect. A person's passion is like a flower; it can take years to develop and grow, but it can be trampled and destroyed by someone else very quickly and easily. It's important to protect a person's passion, rather than be casually cruel and stamp it out.

If you are going about your day doing something you enjoy and someone comes up to you and says **'YOU'RE WEIRD FOR DOING THAT'**, I want you to understand that you are not the problem. The problem is the person who takes time out of their day to go out and try to take someone's smile away. That is disrespectful, and it's something we can all do without in this world.

I also think that if you see someone do this to someone else, you should feel empowered to question them. You can ask them things like, **'WHY DO YOU GET TO DECIDE WHAT IS WEIRD AND WHAT IS NORMAL?'** or, **'I DON'T THINK THEY'RE BOTHERING ANYONE, WHY DOES SOMEONE ENJOYING THEMSELVES HURT YOU SO MUCH?'**

I want you to ask yourself these questions if you encounter someone doing something different that you might find confusing or strange at first.

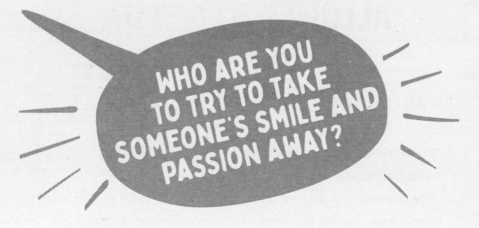

WHO ARE YOU TO TRY TO TAKE SOMEONE'S SMILE AND PASSION AWAY?

Just because something is different, or you haven't seen it before, doesn't mean it is bad.

IF A PERSON IS DOING SOMETHING THEY ENJOY, THEY SHOULD BE ALLOWED TO GET ON WITH ENJOYING IT, AS LONG AS IT DOESN'T HURT ANYONE ELSE.

You should have the freedom to explore and figure out what it is that makes you happy in this life. Your journey will be different from those of the people around you, and your talents and interests will vary from those of everyone else. But when you share your talents with other people it brings out the best in both of you.

Do you ever have moments
when your friend is really excited
about some news, then all of a sudden
you find yourself getting excited too?
Even if you don't really know
what's going on?

I LOVE THAT FEELING.

Seeing a person you like being happy can often make you feel happy as well. Friends bring out the best in each other, and that can be through the things you have in common, but also through the things that are different. If someone's interested in writing they can team up with someone who loves drawing and – **BOOM!** – together they can create a comic book! Or if someone who is really into photography and cameras meets someone who is really into acting, they could make films together!

THE MORE WE SHARE

THE MORE WE LEARN

AND THE MORE WE LEARN,
THE MORE WE

GROW AND DEVELOP

AS PEOPLE

AS A COMMUNITY

AND AS A WORLD

In fact, this idea goes deeper than hobbies and interests — it applies to the bigger differences we have as people. *THINGS LIKE THE COLOUR OF OUR SKIN, OUR GENDER, OUR RELIGION AND WHO WE CHOOSE TO LOVE.* I think we should celebrate those differences, too. I'll give you a small example — I said before that I try my hardest to support women's football and bring it to a bigger audience, and I think that other football fans should try to support it too. Watching Manchester United women's team is different from watching the men's team that I play for, but that difference should be celebrated and championed! They're as much a part of Manchester United as I am.

While women's football was banned for 50 years in the UK, it missed out on a lot of opportunities to grow. I think it's important that everyone who likes football does something — however small — to make the next 50 years of women's football special. Even simple things like watching a game on TV, learning more about your football club's women's team or standing up for women's football if you hear someone say something negative about it can make a huge difference.

I LOVE FOOTBALL BECAUSE IT IS A GAME THAT CAN BE PLAYED BY ANYONE, ABSOLUTELY ANYWHERE IN THE WORLD — ALL YOU NEED IS SOMETHING YOU CAN KICK AROUND, SOMETHING TO BE A GOAL, AND VOILÀ! IT'S A GAME FOR EVERYONE, AND I WANT EVERYONE TO FEEL LIKE THEY ARE WELCOME IN THIS SPACE.

THIS CONCEPT —
OF SUPPORTING AND CELEBRATING SOMEONE'S DIFFERENCE, EVEN IF YOU DON'T NECESSARILY HAVE TO —
IS CALLED ALLYSHIP.

Everyone in this world — including you — has a voice, but unfortunately not everyone's voice is heard by the world. Historically, it has often been the biggest or most powerful groups who have had the loudest voices, so they've been the ones to make the most important decisions about how the world works. That's brought about some good things, but it's also brought some painful things for the people who are not a part of those big groups.

AS A BLACK PERSON, I KNOW THAT RACISM HAS
DENIED A LOT OF OPPORTUNITIES TO PEOPLE WHO
LOOK LIKE ME. FOR LARGE PARTS OF HISTORY, BLACK
PEOPLE AND OTHER ETHNIC MINORITIES HAVE OFTEN
HAD TO LIVE IN A WORLD THAT MADE DECISIONS FOR
THEM, INSTEAD OF BEING ASKED THEIR OPINION ON
THINGS. VERY OFTEN THIS HAS CREATED A WORLD
WHERE MINORITIES DON'T GET TO LIVE WITH EQUAL
RIGHTS, ARE UNABLE TO GO TO GOOD SCHOOLS AND
DON'T HAVE EQUAL ACCESS TO MEDICAL HELP.

Because the loudest voices didn't ask everyone for their opinion, they
created a world that doesn't work for everyone. This means that the
world was built for a certain type of person to succeed. It means there
are things in the world right now that will probably have to change in
order for things to get better for all of us.

I'll give you an example of a positive change that has already been made.
There was a time in English football when some fans didn't want their
team to have Black players, and who even didn't want Black people to go
to football stadiums. Some looked at Black people and thought 'They're
too different from us. They will never understand how football works
here. They'll ruin everything if we let them get involved in our game.'
This is what happens when the loudest voices decide something for
everyone without properly talking to everyone.

But eventually a lot of very good Black footballers from all over the world proved how wrong the old ways of thinking were. White football managers and players understood that Black football players might be different from what came before, but they decided to celebrate that difference, rather than dismiss it. Slowly, football clubs began to understand that if they opened their doors to people from Black backgrounds, the whole club would learn and develop from what we could bring to the game.

On top of that, anti-racism groups like **Kick It Out** helped to change the minds of decision-makers in football and explained that even though there were some differences in footballers from all over the world, a person's skin colour didn't make one group better than another. There's another group called **Nujum** that also works to help football clubs understand and celebrate the beliefs and culture of Muslim footballers, so they can get the proper support they need during Ramadan and other important times in the Islamic calendar.

A lot has changed and football is now more accepting of people who look like me and who have a different religion from me, and most people agree that that is a good thing. There is still a lot of work to be done, but I feel like Black footballers and football fans, along with other ethnic minorities, have more of a voice than they had before, and that voice has helped improve football for everyone. However, there are also other differences that are still not as accepted in the game, and I will do everything in my power to help those voices be heard alongside mine.

IN ORDER FOR THE WORLD TO GET BETTER
— FOR EVERYONE —
WE ALL HAVE TO
USE OUR VOICES
TO LIFT UP EVERYONE ELSE.

To achieve this, everyone will need to pitch in a little bit, and to do that we need to create a space where more people than ever can bring just a little part of themselves to help. All of their talents. All of their personality. And all of their differences too. People find it easier to contribute to things if they feel that they are seen and heard. That's why if someone comes along who has a different voice and says something you've never heard before, it's important to make sure you take time to listen to what they have to say.

WE CAN DO INCREDIBLE THINGS WHEN WE ALL COME TOGETHER.

There's a phrase I want you to say out loud now:

THINGS
DON'T CHANGE
IF THINGS
DON'T CHANGE

It can be a bit complicated at first, which is why I want you to say it out loud. Think about each word as you say it.

The phrase means that in order for things to get better, we often have to do things that are different from what was being done before. A lot of the time that means we have to stop, look at who are making the big decisions in life and ask whether those decisions are working for the people they affect. The answer might be no, and if it is, we have to ask ourselves why.

Before we finish this chapter, I have one final example of how being an ally can help make a positive impact. I started working on the anti-food-poverty project because I felt decisions were being made without listening to those who needed that support the most. When I was a child I was on free school meals and went to Breakfast Club. My mum worked more than one job and tried her hardest to put food on the table, but some days it wasn't enough and she needed help feeding me. I know what it was like to be one of those children who needed those free school meals, and I wanted to be an ally to them, to support them and give them my voice when they weren't heard.

I WANTED TO BE THE PERSON MY FAMILY HAD NEEDED WHEN I WAS YOUNGER.

During the anti-food-poverty project, I wrote a letter on social media that said:

> **THESE CHILDREN ARE THE FUTURE OF THIS COUNTRY. THEY ARE NOT JUST ANOTHER STATISTIC. AND FOR AS LONG AS THEY DON'T HAVE A VOICE, THEY WILL HAVE MINE.**

I tried to use my voice as a megaphone to project the needs of vulnerable families living in the country today. I wanted to ask 'How can I help?', then make sure the biggest audience possible heard what those people had to say, so we could all get involved and go about helping them together. I asked for allyship from people all over the country, to come together and use their voices to help these children. To help get the message across to powerful decision-makers that more needed to be done. Over time, all of those many megaphones of allyship helped the message become louder and louder, to the point where the government decided to provide funding and support to the families, like mine had been, who were previously going unheard.

YOU ARE ONLY JUST COMING INTO DISCOVERING YOUR VOICE BUT I WANT YOU TO UNDERSTAND IT HAS A POWER THAT CAN CHANGE THE WORLD – NOT ONLY FOR YOU BUT FOR THE PEOPLE AROUND YOU – IF YOU CHOOSE TO BE AN ALLY.

THAT SOUNDS LIKE A LOT OF PRESSURE, RIGHT?

I'll admit that being an ally isn't always an easy thing, but sometimes trying to change the world can be as simple as seeing someone drop some litter and asking them to put it in the bin instead, to be an ally to environmentalists. Some days being an ally means being the only one to stand up for someone who needs your help at school, but other days it can be as simple as giving a thumbs up to a stranger in the street who looks like they are having a bad day. Being an ally can be doing something small for different people in your life, but it is so, so, so important to how we get along and thrive together as a community.

Once you recognise that there is no such thing as normal, you can accept all of the little differences that make us unique and special, and then you realise that those special parts of us should be celebrated. Being an ally is that extra bit of encouragement that helps people who need support carry on when things are dark. It's someone speaking out for someone else. It's cheering that person on, helping someone pick themselves up when they get knocked down, and connecting with someone who is feeling lonely.

LIKE I SAID IN THE LAST CHAPTER, IT'S NOT 'US' AND 'THEM', BUT 'ALL OF US, TOGETHER, DOING OUR OWN THING'. Allyship is understanding that we should never be in conflict with each other, and that the world is better and more interesting when we don't place limitations on ourselves or other people, but champion each other instead.

Unfortunately, the world isn't kind to everyone, so to build a world that is we need to be kind to each other in as many small moments as possible. That means standing up for each other, learning from each other and exchanging ideas wherever possible, to empower everyone, and especially those people whose voices aren't always heard.

Like I said before, a person's passion is like a flower; it can take years to develop and grow, but it can be trampled by someone else very quickly and easily. Even to this day, I still do little doodles of Donatello in my notepads when I'm passing the time. I feel comfortable doing it, because of what happened all of those years before, when my friends told me not to be embarrassed by my drawings.

And if we all work our hardest to look after our own flowers and protect other people's as well, we can grow the most amazing gardens that can spread all over the world. A world that is full of different passions and interests, different religions, different types of love and so much more.

I'd like a world where people feel like they can show off these parts of themselves and be celebrated for it. A person should never have to hide who they are; if we all celebrate differences, everyone can feel more comfortable being themselves, all the time.

CHAPTER FOUR
ACTION POINTS

1. WHAT ARE YOUR FLOWERS?

What are you passionate about? What makes you smile, even if someone else thinks it's uncool or weird? Grab a piece of paper and draw a picture of some of your passions! It could be you playing a sport, or a musical instrument, or hanging out with your friends.

2. BE AN ALLY

Allyship means supporting and celebrating someone's difference. It's about championing the rights and freedoms of people being discriminated against when you belong to a different group. For example, men can be allies to women by fighting for women's rights, and white people can be allies to people of colour by educating themselves about racism.

Above all, being an ally means *listening* more than talking and doing what you can to lift up the voices of people who aren't being heard.

Think of unfair situations you see around you in your daily life. What are three ways you can be an ally for someone else? It could be a sibling, a friend or anyone in your local community. Remember when I said that my friends stood up for me when people tried to make fun of me? Are there ways you've had other people step up and be allies for you?

3. SHOW OFF YOUR GARDEN

Together the different flowers of our passions combine to create beautiful gardens across the world! How amazing is that?

Think of all the different passions the members of your family have, or the passions of your closest friends, or another group you belong to. Draw what the 'garden' of these different passions would look like on a piece of paper. You can draw the passions as different flowers – a football sunflower, or a music note rose – or you can simply draw different symbols representing various activities, interests and topics.

Now compare your 'garden' to the drawing of your passions above. Take a moment to celebrate all the different passions the people around you bring to your garden!

HOW TO MAKE A

CHANGE

5

HEY MARCUS, WHAT MADE YOU START WORKING AGAINST FOOD POVERTY?

IT'S A QUESTION I GET ASKED A LOT.

It's also a question I still don't know how to answer properly. I had done some charitable campaigns in Manchester before, particularly to help homeless people, but the child food poverty project was really different. What started off as a small idea in the early spring of 2020 grew into something massive, affecting millions of people's lives, and ended up with me talking to the Prime Minister! So many unbelievable things happened in 2020 that it can be sort of strange to say it out loud to someone.

SO WHAT I'LL DO WITH YOU IS WRITE SOME OF IT DOWN.

It all started in March 2020 when a boy wrote me a letter asking if I would judge a poetry competition for World Book Day at his school.

The boy has a hearing impediment and communicates via sign language, and he goes to school with the help of sensory support services in Manchester.

> Sensory support services work by giving advice and training to people who are deaf, hard-of-hearing or visually impaired, and also to the people around them, like teachers, parents and others in the community. These services can play a really valuable role in helping to improve people's communications skills and give people like my letter-writing friend an extra boost when needed.

When I got his letter I immediately wanted to help, and I thought the best way for me to judge the poetry competition would be for me to learn some British sign language so that I could talk to him in a way that he would find comfortable. After all, if he was going to write such beautiful poems for me to read, I thought I should at least be able to say thank you!

Learning sign language was really fun. I learned how to say **'Good morning'**, by holding up a thumb and tapping both sides of my chest.

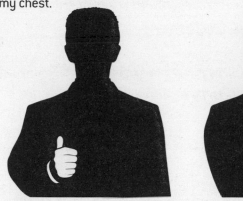

I learned how to say **'Well done'**, too. That's done by doing a thumbs up in each hand before rolling your hands around each other in a circle. (It's a little trickier than good morning – the first time I tried it, my instructor told me that I had accidentally given the gesture for milk!)

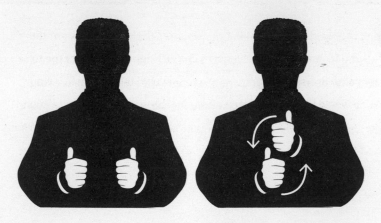

I wasn't playing professional football at the time, as I was recovering from injuries to my back and my foot. I was finding the rest period difficult — not being allowed to play football or train with my teammates was tough — and I was feeling quite down.

I FELT LIKE I'D LOST MY PASSION. I SPENT A LOT OF TIME IN BETWEEN INJURY RECOVERY SESSIONS SITTING AT HOME WONDERING WHAT TO DO WITH MYSELF. (LIKE I SAID AT THE START OF THIS BOOK, I'M NOT THAT GOOD AT TAKING BREAKS!)

But judging that competition brought out a different passion in me. When I was injured, I missed working as part of a team and helping get things done, but the letter showed me that there were so many more teams I could help and be a part of. It made me realise that I wanted to give something back and help out the next generation.

And I started to think about other ways I could help children who were growing up in my local area.

It wasn't too long after that poetry competition that the first lockdown happened – you probably remember how strange it was, when all the schools and nearly all of the shops were shut, and we had to stay at home all the time.

I really got to thinking about what sort of help my family might have needed if I was still at school during that time. The more I thought about it, the more I wondered if there might be families out there who needed help with their food shopping.

As I said before, when I was a child I was on free school meals, and the thought of schools being closed and children missing out on Breakfast Club and other meals they got when they were at school worried me.

IF YOU'RE A CHILD ON FREE SCHOOL MEALS, I WANT TO SAY HELLO! I USED TO BE ON FREE SCHOOL MEALS TOO! AND I DON'T WANT YOU TO EVER THINK THAT BEING ON FREE SCHOOL MEALS MAKES YOU 'NOT NORMAL'. REMEMBER, THERE IS NO SUCH THING AS NORMAL (LIKE I SAID IN CHAPTER 3), AND YOU SHOULD NEVER BE MADE TO FEEL BAD ABOUT YOUR BACKGROUND. HOW YOU EAT YOUR MEALS IS LESS IMPORTANT THAN THE FACT THAT YOU ARE EATING AND BEING LOOKED AFTER. NEVER FORGET THAT.

If you're not on free school meals you might not know what they are, so I'll explain it very quickly. Free school meals vouchers are available to some families in the UK who have children between the ages 5 and 19. Families can apply for the vouchers, and once that request for help is approved, the government sends the vouchers to the child's school so that they can be exchanged for food during lunch. In a perfect world, we wouldn't need free school meals vouchers and every child would have enough food at home. But in this world free school meals are really important and are a much-needed way to make sure that as many children as possible in the UK get at least one nutritious meal a day.

As a child on free school meals, all I could think was that if I'd been a child when lockdown hit, my family would have been in a bit of trouble. I didn't want other children to be going hungry, so I started to do some research with a few charities to see what help we could offer families over lockdown.

That was the point when I spoke to an amazing charity called FareShare, who I still work with today. They are the largest charity in the UK that is getting food to those in need, and they help around 11,000 primary schools and smaller charities across the country. They're really good at working with volunteers and big supermarkets to make sure good food that might otherwise go to waste ends up going to people who need help with their food shopping.

By talking to them I realised how much support families across the UK need – I found out there are about **4.2 million children** in the UK who need help getting food every day. That made me really upset, and I started to realise how much work had to be done.

When I was a child, people in my local area stepped in to support my family and others when we needed food. I've already told you about Greg in Chapter 2, who helped my family when times were tough, and I started to think, 'Wouldn't it be great if every child had their own version of Greg?' Many children up and down the country need someone like that in their lives, someone who could help with meals if things got difficult, no questions asked.

So I knew I wanted to make a change, but I also knew I couldn't do it all by myself.

FINDING YOUR VOICE AND PURPOSE IN LIFE IS ONE THING, BUT, VERY OFTEN, WHEN IT IS TIME TO USE THAT VOICE AND MAKE A CHANGE YOU WILL NEED A BIT OF TEAMWORK TO MAKE THINGS HAPPEN.

AND THIS IS THE PART OF THE STORY WHERE PEOPLE LIKE YOU COME IN.

After talking to FareShare I realised that one way I could help was by donating both my money and my time to the charity, but I also learned that I could make a **much bigger difference** if I asked other people to help me. So even as I started working with FareShare to help get food to families in need, I also started to ask for help on social media. Throughout the spring of 2020 I asked members of the public to donate time and/or a few pennies to their local food bank where they could, and to simply talk about an issue that had not been addressed in some time.

I didn't expect to see so many people join in and help us — hundreds of people got in touch with FareShare and other similar charities to ask how they could get involved.
Some people volunteered at their local food banks, while others donated food and money to these charities. Some people worked to raise money, using their talents for the greater good, while others wrote letters to people in government to raise the issue.

Our initial aim was to help 40,000 people with free meals, but thanks to *your* help we ended up providing

OVER 3,000,000 MEALS

to those in need by the start of June that year. That was amazing, but what happened next really blew me away.

YOU SEE, EVEN THOUGH WE WERE ALL AT HOME DURING THE LOCKDOWN, WE WERE COMING TO THE END OF THE SCHOOL YEAR AND I WAS CONCERNED ABOUT WHAT WOULD HAPPEN WHEN THE GOVERNMENT STOPPED GIVING VOUCHERS TO CHILDREN ON FREE SCHOOL MEALS OVER THE SUMMER HOLIDAYS.

We were building real momentum, but as spring turned to summer, I knew that children would soon stop getting support via free school meals, as the scheme tends to pause over the summer holidays. I thought the best way to express my concern would be to write a letter and ask for help. So on 15 June 2020, I wrote a letter explaining just how many people in the country needed help and sent it to all members of parliament and put it on social media. In the letter I described my own experiences as a child, so that people could better understand what it was like to grow up needing that sort of help. I didn't want to ask for sympathy for myself, I just wanted to make as many people as possible aware of how much help was needed for the next generation. I asked the government to extend the free school meals scheme over the summer holidays to make sure everyone got the assistance they needed during a difficult time.

I hoped that parents and people all over the UK would see that letter, see what myself and the team at FareShare were doing, and then decide that they also wanted to make a change and join the team we were building to get the free school meals scheme extended.

Before I posted that letter on social media, I was worried that people would try to dismiss me and say what I was asking for wasn't realistic. But what really shocked me was how many people wanted to help. They retweeted and shared my letter on social media, and its message ended up being discussed on the news that day. People also joined me in asking the government to extend the free school meals scheme.

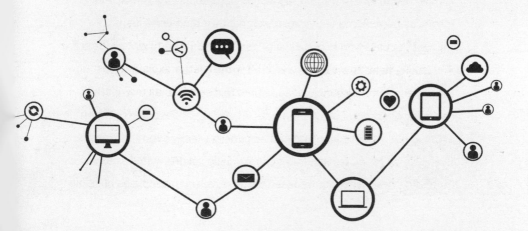

The day after I posted that letter I went to train with Manchester United, and in the afternoon I got a message telling me that someone very important was going to call me later. I thought that was a bit odd – normally when someone I know tries to call me, they wait until after I've finished training so I can properly answer. If someone tries to call me when I'm at training it is usually an emergency, so it was odd to get a message that sounded like an emergency but also told me to wait. But as the afternoon went on I got some text messages that explained what was happening.

THE GOVERNMENT HAD DECIDED TO EXTEND THE FREE SCHOOL MEALS SCHEME OVER THE SUMMER HOLIDAYS. AND WHAT'S MORE, THE PRIME MINISTER WANTED TO CALL ME UP AND EXPLAIN WHY.

It was a little surreal talking to the Prime Minister. I've met famous people before, but that's normally through football, so this was a bit different! He explained that everyone coming together to take action by volunteering at the food banks, writing letters to MPs and making donations to charity had made the government pay attention and had convinced them to extend the free school meals scheme over the summer holidays.

I am forever grateful to the boy who wrote me that letter, FareShare and people from across the UK for what they have done over the past two years. Millions of people up and down the country helped families all over the UK to get the sort of food aid they needed during a really difficult time. This journey is not yet complete, but I'm really proud of how we came together and started to make a change.

MY JOURNEY TO MAKING A CHANGE STARTED WITH ME DOING ONE SMALL THING – JUDGING A POETRY COMPETITION – BEFORE I FOUND MY PASSION AND PURSUED IT.

It was important for me to tell you this story so you can see that making a positive change doesn't happen overnight, and that you don't have to do it by yourself. I didn't wake up one morning and just say to myself 'I'm going to fix everything'. I think when people try to make a positive change it happens gradually, bit by bit. You notice one thing in the world that seems a bit off, then you try to learn about it. Once you've learned about it a bit, you might have a moment where you think,

CAN WE DO ANYTHING TO CHANGE THAT?

AND THEN THE JOURNEY BEGINS . . .

Very often, your journey will start from something you already know. I came to food campaigning because I wanted to do something to help children, and helping children on free school meals made sense as I had been one of them. I knew what it felt like to be one of those kids.

Take a moment to think about the things you are already interested in.

Do you like football?

Maybe you could make a change in your local area by trying to get more footballs into your school so there are enough for everyone to be able to play. Or maybe you could look into making sure more people have a safe and clean area to play football games after school. Or maybe you could help champion women's football.

Do you ride a bicycle?

Can you do something to help road safety in your local area? Or can you make sure everyone in your class knows where to go to get their bike fixed if it gets broken?

Do you like helping others?

Is there a food drive you can support in your local area, so you can help those who need meals, like my family once did?

Don't worry if you don't know how to help and make a change yet.

ALL CHANGE COMES ABOUT FROM ONE SMALL STEP.

Even if you think you don't have anything to contribute, just wanting to help can go a very long way in making things get better. There's no shame in asking loads of questions when you start, either. Everyone — and I mean everyone — starts their journey from a place of interest, then that moves on to a place of knowledge. It's ok if you don't know exactly how you can start to improve things when you set out.

What's more important is that you know you want things to get better. That you are willing to put yourself out there to make a change.

BECAUSE SO MUCH OF MAKING A CHANGE COMES FROM A PLACE OF <u>VULNERABILITY</u> – WHERE YOU LEAVE YOUR COMFORT ZONE AND OPEN UP PARTS OF YOURSELF FOR THE REST OF THE WORLD TO SEE.

It can be difficult to admit you think there is a problem with how the world around you works. It can be difficult to admit that the way something is done isn't the best way of doing it, especially if you don't immediately have an answer for how to do it better. It can also be difficult to admit you need help in making a change. Because that's where the real big changes happen; not by you working by yourself, but by going to other people and other groups and saying,

'DO YOU WANT TO WORK TOGETHER? I THINK WE CAN DO SOMETHING SPECIAL IF WE DO.'

I WAS NERVOUS WHEN WE FIRST STARTED ON THE FOOD POVERTY JOURNEY. I THOUGHT PEOPLE WERE GOING TO REJECT MY CALLS FOR HELP OR SAY THAT BECAUSE I WAS A FOOTBALLER I 'DIDN'T KNOW WHAT I WAS TALKING ABOUT', BECAUSE FOOD POVERTY IS SUCH A COMPLICATED SUBJECT. BUT THE WAY I SAW IT, THE REWARD OF HELPING ONE PERSON WAS WORTH ANY CRITICISM OTHERS COULD GIVE ME.

When I wrote that letter, I was worried about what people might say about my childhood. My mum didn't want anyone to know the trouble my family had putting food on the table when I was growing up, so I was a bit concerned about telling that story to millions of people. In the end, through talking to my mum, I realised that I had to share my story to help others. Being vulnerable and talking about a low moment in our lives was worth it to make sure people around us had a better future.

Thankfully, people listened to my story, which made it easier for them to listen to the stories of other families. I know it can be hard to ask people for help, but something I've realised in these past few years is that there are a lot of very kind people in this world who want to help — all you have to do is ask them. If there has been pain in your life, I'm sorry, but I hope that one day you feel enough courage to want to make the world a better place. My experience as a child made me want to create a world where the next generation of children wouldn't need to worry so much about free school meals vouchers.

YOUR STORY AND YOUR JOURNEY IS AN IMPORTANT ONE,

AND WHEN YOU CHOOSE TO TELL IT, IT WILL ONE DAY HELP TO

SHAPE THE FUTURE

OF OTHER PEOPLE WHO ARE STILL ON THEIR JOURNEYS.

THE REWARD OF HELPING ONE PERSON, OR HELPING MAKE A CHANGE — HOWEVER SMALL — WILL BE FAR GREATER THAN WHAT ANYONE ELSE CAN SAY TO TRY TO BRING YOU DOWN.

Making a change takes a lot of listening, learning and applying yourself. And then reapplying yourself if you've made a mistake, or if the situation has changed. You might have heard your teacher use the phrase:

ROME WASN'T BUILT IN A DAY

It means that big, world-changing tasks don't happen overnight. You have to put in work and effort, and keep on trying when things go wrong.

(And even if something good looks like it's happened overnight, that normally happens as the result of loads, and I mean LOADS, of hard work in the weeks before that you haven't seen going on!)

Making a change can be a long process, so it's important to have a good team around you to help you stay grounded. The world is big, and it can be frightening to go out there and try to change things, so I always make sure I have a good group of people around me who've got my back. People I can get advice from, and people who can help me celebrate the small joys on my journey, too.

Along the way, I needed a lot of help from experts (like FareShare) and others (like you, reading this) before I could build a team that could make a change.

It wasn't all plain sailing. We encountered a lot of difficulties, and even though we achieved a lot we still understand that we have a long way to go if we want to keep making effective changes in the world.

Your journey might have similar steps.

PROGRESS ISN'T A STRAIGHT LINE, AND THERE WILL BE UPS AND DOWNS ALONG THE WAY.

Don't worry, though, I'm not saying it's your job to go out and help millions of people starting tomorrow! But what I would like you to understand is that there will come a point in your life where you realise you have a voice and a passion, and then you might start trying to use that voice to make a change in the world around you.

FINDING OUT THAT YOU HAVE A VOICE IS ONE OF THE MOST EMPOWERING THINGS YOU WILL EVER EXPERIENCE. USING THAT VOICE TO BRING ABOUT CHANGE CAN BE SCARY AT FIRST, BUT TAKE HEART IN KNOWING THAT THERE IS NOTHING WRONG WITH TRYING TO MAKE THINGS BETTER, AND KNOW THAT YOU WILL NEVER BE ALONE IN YOUR JOURNEY FOR PROGRESS.

My work trying to make a change still isn't finished, and if I get frustrated about that my friends, family and colleagues always remind me of where I was in February 2020, and to think about all of the good things we have achieved together so far. Because positive change happens bit by bit, it can sometimes feel like you're not making any progress when you actually are. So always make sure you take breaks during your journey; not just to make sure things are going ok, but also so you can reflect on how far you have come.

I want you to finish reading this chapter and not think about all of the changes you have to make immediately, but about what might be possible a few years from now, if you commit to making a change – however small – in your area and start working with a group of like-minded people.

Trust me, once you start seeing your impact on the world and your ability to do good within it, you'll want to do it again and again, and again . . .

YOU HAVE A VOICE IN THIS WORLD AND ONCE YOU START USING IT TO MAKE A CHANGE, YOU CAN DO INCREDIBLE THINGS.

CHAPTER FIVE

ACTION POINTS

1. WE CAN CHANGE THE WORLD. TOGETHER.

Isn't it amazing all the ways we can work together to make an impact and change the world? This is even more true with the modern tools we have to reach each other, such as the internet and social media – like I used when I was first reaching out about starting my food programme!

Even before social media, people have been protesting inequality for hundreds of years. They've organised big groups of people in what's called **social movements**. Through social movements, people contact their government, protest in rallies and marches, sign petitions, boycott various companies (which means they refuse to buy things from them) who treat people unequally, and even run for government themselves! All these different ways of fighting for what someone believes in are known as *activism*, and the people who do it are called *activists*.

There are many examples of social movements: workers fighting for their rights, women fighting for the right to vote in the 19th Century, the civil rights movement in the US in the 1950s and 60s which fought for the rights of Black people, as well as the Stonewall Rebellion in New York City, which fought for the rights of LGBTQ+ people. For every cause you can think of, there has probably been a social movement filled with people **trying to make the world better**. Even something like the weekend – where you get Saturday and Sunday away from work and school – came about due to the efforts of factory workers in the early 1900s!

Think about something you care about in your area, and then do some research into learning more about it. You can ask your teachers or a parent for help with your research. Very often, activists learn about the work that happened before them and then look into how they might work with others in future.

Grab a piece of paper and write out the following sentences, filling in the gaps:

- ◑ I am really interested in making ⁓⁓⁓⁓⁓⁓⁓⁓⁓ better in my area.

- ◑ The reason I am interested is ⁓⁓⁓⁓⁓⁓⁓⁓ .

- ◑ I've been doing some learning and I have found out that the history of ⁓⁓⁓⁓⁓⁓⁓⁓⁓⁓ is ⁓⁓⁓⁓⁓⁓⁓⁓⁓⁓⁓⁓⁓⁓ .

- ◑ If I want ⁓⁓⁓⁓⁓⁓⁓⁓⁓ to get better in my area, I could do ⁓⁓⁓⁓⁓⁓⁓⁓⁓⁓ .

2. TRY, TRY AND TRY AGAIN

Remember how I said making a change can be a long process? Just
like how learning is a gradual process where you'll sometimes make
mistakes, trying to make a difference is a process
that can take a while. There are always
ways we can make the world better. And
sometimes it can be really hard, and feel
frustrating, to wonder if we're actually
making a difference. But when we work
together, making sure we take breaks for
our health while others fight on, and then fight on
when *those* people need a break, we help give each other
the energy we need to keep on going until we've achieved our goals.

Nelson Mandela is one of the most famous activists in the whole world.
He spent his entire life fighting for racial justice – fighting for equal
rights for Black people and people of colour – in his home country of
South Africa. Mandela was born in 1918, and he lived under a racist
government who created a policy where white people were treated
better than people of colour in every aspect of life.

Mandela and others who wanted to stop racism started fighting back. They organised protests and eventually got people around the world to stand against the South African government throughout the 1970s and '80s. The government arrested Nelson and many others. They sent him to prison in 1963, where he was forced to stay for a whole 27 years.

Mandela would have been forced to stay in prison for the rest of his life if the racist government had its way. But because the activists never gave up, South African society — overwhelmingly Black and other groups of people of colour — succeeded in rejecting the violent racism that had been forced upon them. Nelson Mandela then went on to become South Africa's first Black president in 1994!

I say all of this to remind you that when people stay united against hatred and keep trying to make a change, they can *move mountains.*

Nelson Mandela once said,

'IT ALWAYS SEEMS IMPOSSIBLE UNTIL IT IS DONE.'

It's something I think about a lot. The road is long, and sometimes hard, but I want you to try your best to keep your determination to make your world a better place, no matter what may happen.

For this activity, I want you to write some messages to yourself, which you can come back to when your journey gets difficult.

What's your version of
'It always seems impossible until it is done'...?

Start off by writing your name on a piece of paper, and then write:

'I CAN DO AMAZING THINGS.'

'I'M GOING TO WORK AS PART OF A TEAM TO HELP MAKE THE WORLD A BETTER PLACE.'

'SOMETHING I REALLY CARE ABOUT IS . . . . '

'SOMETHING I'D LIKE TO CHANGE ABOUT THE WORLD AROUND ME IS . . . . '

'WHEN THINGS GET DIFFICULT, I TRY TO REMIND MYSELF THAT I AM LOVED, THAT PEOPLE ARE ROOTING FOR ME AND, WHILE THINGS ARE DIFFICULT NOW, THEY WON'T BE DIFFICULT FOREVER.'

BOUNCING
BACK

6

AS A FOOTBALLER I TRY MY BEST TO WIN EVERY SINGLE GAME WITH MY TEAM.

I work extremely hard in my training, both on the pitch and in the gym, and I have to make sure I eat right and get enough sleep so my body is at 100% before I play. When I'm playing for Manchester United I spend a couple of hours every week in classroom sessions, studying the upcoming opposition to make sure I know as much as possible about my next opponent, and I go over video footage of my own performances at home to see what I can do to improve and help the team.

(THAT'S RIGHT, FOOTBALLERS HAVE HOMEWORK TOO — YOU NEVER STOP LEARNING!)

EVERY DAY I DO EVERYTHING IN MY POWER TO
GET MY MIND AND BODY TO A PLACE WHERE I CAN
PERFORM AT MY MAXIMUM AND HELP MY TEAM TO
WIN. I TRY TO TAKE THOSE PRINCIPLES OVER TO
MY WORK AWAY FROM FOOTBALL, TOO. When I'm doing
my charity work and campaigning against food poverty, I do my best
to read up on all the facts and talk to experts so I can make the most
knowledgeable decisions in order to help people. I talk to people who
work for the government, food charities, supermarkets and the people
who run food banks to understand more about how we get food to those
in need in the UK.

But despite all this preparation, I'm not always successful. I've lost some
of the biggest games a footballer can ever play in their career, and there
have been times during my work to help kids when the ideas we came up
with to help people were rejected by those in power. Even today, despite
all of our hard work, we know there are still some families who aren't
getting the support they need.

KNOWING THAT YOU CAN TRY YOUR BEST BUT STILL FAIL IS REALLY DIFFICULT.

I believe that you are capable of amazing things, but it's important for me to say that there will be days when you have prepared as much as you can, and you have the best intentions, but you will still make mistakes.

And that will be ok.

KNOWING YOU'VE MADE A MISTAKE IS A TERRIBLE FEELING — TRUST ME, I KNOW. BUT JUST BECAUSE YOU'VE MADE A MISTAKE, YOU'RE NOT LESS THAN WHAT YOU WERE BEFORE.

Throughout my life, I've made mistakes and I've had things go wrong for me. At school, I've forgotten to hand in my homework. On more than one occasion I got in trouble with my mum because I scuffed the shoes she'd bought me because I was always kicking a ball. As an adult, I've dropped and broken my phone, my laptop, my favourite mug for cups of tea. I've read a map wrong and gone in the wrong direction on a car journey, and I've turned up to meet my friends and ended up in the wrong place, or at the wrong time.

On the football side of things, I've made mistakes in my shooting, in my dribbling, in my passing. Sometimes I'll be playing a game and I'll realise I've been standing in the wrong place for just a fraction too long. I made a mistake in one of the biggest games in English football, where millions of people from around the world were watching, and people were really upset with me.

BUT THE WAY I SEE IT, NONE OF THESE MISTAKES
DEFINE WHO I AM. WHAT'S MORE IMPORTANT IS
WHAT I DO NEXT, AND HOW I REACT TO MAKING
THAT MISTAKE.

And let me tell you now, I don't give up on what I'm trying to do. Instead,
I try to think of it as a learning opportunity, so I can grow and come out
better on the other side. Without the mistakes I've made in life, I wouldn't
be the person or the player that I am today.

There's this phrase a lot of coaches use in football training:

THERE'S NO SHAME IN BEING KNOCKED DOWN. IT'S STAYING DOWN THAT'S THE PROBLEM

and I think it is one of the most important lessons I've ever been taught.

You're constantly learning as a footballer — how to adapt to the opposition, how to maximise your skills and how to balance out any weaknesses that you or a teammate may have. Football works because people make mistakes, and every team has a chance of winning, no matter who they're playing against. Every defeat on the football field is a chance to learn something, and the best thing about football is there is nearly always a game right around the corner where you can apply your new learnings. The most unexpected person could score one of the best goals you've ever seen and shock the world, and even the best teams ever in Premier League history have conceded goals and lost matches on their way to winning the trophy.

> **WHAT SEPARATES THE BEST FOOTBALL TEAMS AND THE BEST FOOTBALL PLAYERS IS HOW THEY REACT TO A MISTAKE. THEY DON'T GIVE UP, EVEN WHEN SOMETHING GOES WRONG FOR THEM.**

MAKING MISTAKES IS UNAVOIDABLE.

That's not me trying to be negative, but it's important for you to know so that when you make a mistake you can be kind to yourself and learn from it, and, just as importantly, when someone else makes a mistake you can be kind to them. If someone knows they've made a mistake and will need to try harder next time, be kind, empathise and let them learn, just as you would want someone to help you get back up when you've done something wrong.

Here's a non-footballing way that I think about it. Have you ever seen someone make pancakes? The first one out of the frying pan is nearly always the worst one. It'll be too small, too big, overcooked, or the wrong shape. No one likes eating the first pancake, but it is the **MOST IMPORTANT ONE** because it shows you how you can make what comes next better.

If the first pancake is too small then the person cooking knows to add more batter for the next one.

If it's overcooked and burnt then the chef knows to turn the heat down.

THE NEXT TIME YOU SEE SOMEONE MAKE PANCAKES, WATCH HOW THE PILE GETS BETTER OVER TIME.

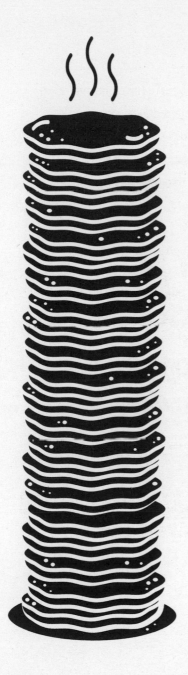

Mistakes are part of the process of making a good batch of pancakes, just like how they are part of the process in your own personal journey.

THE TRICK TO MAKING GOOD PANCAKES ISN'T TO AVOID MAKING A MISTAKE, THE TRICK IS NOT TO GIVE UP WHEN THE FIRST ONE ISN'T SO GOOD.

Just like there has to be rain to make a rainbow, sometimes mistakes have to be made before we can make a change. You might try to learn more about the world around you, try to ask a question, or try to help someone and make a mistake while you are doing it. It's natural, especially if you're attempting something that has never been done before, but that doesn't mean you should stop trying.

Just like with pancakes, often a breakthrough will come directly after a mistake because you can apply what you learned when you try again. And the best way to correct a mistake is to learn from it, and so that we won't make the same one twice.

IT'S ALL PART OF A PROCESS OF LEARNING AND UNDERSTANDING.

Remember at the start of this chapter when I said I have homework as a footballer, where I look over my own performances? I try to follow a thought process whenever it is time for me to go over the mistakes I have in my own game. Have a read through this list and see if you can use it if you ever have to go over your own mistakes.

- **Don't be afraid to try something different,** otherwise you might never learn anything new.

- **Don't worry about making mistakes.** They test your limits and help you figure out what you are good at and what you are less good at.

- **Learn from your mistakes** so you don't make the same one twice. You will make new mistakes as you learn and grow.

- **Own up to your mistakes.** One of the best things you can ever do after slipping up is apologise to people around you. It's the first step in beginning a healing process that will help you move on. (There's a quick saying for this, 'If you mess up, fess up', and if you're into football you might see us wave and give each other a thumbs up after a bad pass. That's our way of owning our mistakes and quickly apologising to each other.)

- **Don't be afraid to go over your mistakes soon afterwards.** That way you can understand what went wrong and work out how to do better next time.

That last one can be really hard, but it's linked to the previous point: a key part of owning your mistakes is being able to ask **why** it happened in the first place.

DID YOU TRY TO DO SOMETHING TOO QUICKLY?

DID YOU DO IT TOO SLOWLY?

WERE YOUR INTENTIONS RIGHT BUT YOU SAID SOMETHING TOO HARSHLY?

DID YOU ATTEMPT TO DO SOMETHING BY YOURSELF WHEN YOU COULD HAVE ASKED FOR OR WAITED FOR HELP?

Mistakes happen for loads of reasons, but that doesn't mean there are loads of things wrong with what you tried to do. It might be a bit embarrassing to go over low moments in your life, but if you take time to understand what happened you'll learn how to do better in the future.

I try my hardest to remember those points whenever something hasn't worked out for me. And not just with things like spilling my tea, getting lost or missing a shot on goal, but also with more complicated mistakes. Like, maybe I've told a joke that I thought would be funny, but instead I've just ended up upsetting one of my friends. It can be uncomfortable to know you've hurt someone you care about, which is why it's important to remember that making mistakes is all part of a process.

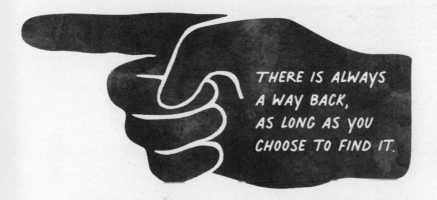

THERE IS ALWAYS A WAY BACK, AS LONG AS YOU CHOOSE TO FIND IT.

And remember that you need to keep the right people around you to help you learn, people who will allow you to recognise your mistakes and who will encourage you to correct them.

In your journey to find your voice and make a difference, you will make mistakes and say or do the wrong thing at times, but that doesn't mean the end of your journey. Just because you have stumbled, it doesn't mean you should stop trying. Any journey of growth will have a few low points along the way, but what's most important is how we bounce back and get back onto the right path.

And I think we should always choose to come back from our mistakes. To apologise to the people we've hurt. To ask them how we could make things better for next time.

DON'T LET A MISTAKE BOX YOU IN AND HAVE YOU SHY AWAY FROM THINGS IN LIFE.

LIFE IS MEANT TO BE FULL OF EXPLORATION, OF FINDING YOURSELF, DISCOVERING YOUR VOICE AND USING THAT VOICE TO IMPROVE YOURSELF AND YOUR SURROUNDINGS. MISTAKES SHOULDN'T LEAD YOU TO BE WITHDRAWN AND MAKE YOURSELF SMALLER, BUT THEY CAN BE A GOOD WAY TO LEARN HOW TO PROPERLY CHANNEL THE THINGS YOU WANT TO DO BETTER NEXT TIME.

As you grow up you come to understand that you don't have to follow up on every single idea that pops into your head, because that might not be the best thing for you or the people around you. The things that look amazing to you today might not be the best a day, a week or even a month down the line when you've thought about it some more. This can be tricky when you're surrounded by things that can be really tempting, or you're in a situation where maybe you feel the best way to fit in is to go along with what everyone else is doing or saying. Don't feel bad if you've made a mistake like this in the past. I've told a lot of you this before, but when I was younger I used to play a game with my mates called 'Knock a Door and Run' – where you'd go up to a stranger's front door, ring the doorbell a few times and then run away before they could answer.

It probably wasn't the best thing for all of us to do around our area at the time, but we would do it anyway because we were bored. But as we got older and started to think about the impact of us doing this to everyone in our street, and who we were bothering, we stopped. My friends didn't want to be the group of kids who caused trouble.

Maybe you've made decisions because you were bored, or because someone told you it'd be funny, or maybe you did a thing for reasons you can't explain yet, but recognising that it wasn't the right decision is the first step. Don't ever feel you are trapped in making a bad decision. But if for some reason you do end up making a bad decision, don't let it define who you are.

ONE BAD MISTAKE DOESN'T MAKE YOU A BAD PERSON.

PEOPLE ARE COMPLEX, AND WE ALL MAKE DECISIONS EVERY DAY THAT AFFECT OURSELVES AND OTHER PEOPLE. IDEALLY, WE'D ALL LIKE TO LIVE LIVES FULL OF GOOD DECISIONS, BUT SOMETIMES WE GET IT WRONG. THAT'S PART OF BEING HUMAN.

The important bit for me is to make sure you don't get comfortable with your mistakes, that you never see the impact of a mistake and think it's someone else's problem to fix. Where I grew up it could be easy for you to get into trouble with a teacher, or the police, and get known as 'The Bad Kid' or 'The Problem Child', but the way I see it, a person's reputation doesn't have to be fixed. You don't have to live your life as 'The Bad Person' just because someone said you are, or because they think you come from a bad place, or because you did a bad thing once (or even twice or three times!).

IF YOU WANT TO MAKE A CHANGE IN SOMETHING — EVEN YOURSELF —
YOU CAN DO IT.
IT JUST TAKES TIME, AND TRUST IN YOURSELF TO DO SO.

What helps you bounce back are the people around you who can offer advice and help with your decisions, as well as supporting you when you choose to take a positive step. For me, those people are my mum, my brothers and my sisters – I've always asked for their advice whenever I get stuck, and their perspective helps me a lot because I know they've always got my back. My friends help me out as well, always reminding me that mistakes happen and that I'm not always going to get things right all the time, but so long as I keep trying and keep learning, and keep being respectful of the people around me, then I can keep improving and keep doing the good things I want to do in the world.

I try to give that support back to my friends and family, too. When they're trying to come back from a mistake it's important for me to help them like they would help me. If you can create a cycle like that for the people around you, then you're on your way to building a good system of support and forgiveness.

The important part is forgiving yourself when you've made a mistake, as that is often the first step that's needed to bounce back and try again.

SAY YOUR NAME OUT LOUD RIGHT NOW.

SAY 'I AM ALLOWED TO MAKE MISTAKES.'

SAY 'AND I WILL TRY NOT TO BE SO HARD ON MYSELF WHEN THOSE MISTAKES HAPPEN.' (THIS IS THE FORGIVENESS PART!)

SAY 'IT'S NOT THE WORST THING IN THE WORLD IF I MAKE A MISTAKE, SO LONG AS I TRY MY BEST TO LEARN FROM IT AND CORRECT THINGS FOR NEXT TIME.'

I want you to remember these words when something goes wrong in your life. And I also want you to remember them if someone makes a mistake that ends up hurting you. You aren't the only person who is going to read this book, and there are loads of people – just like you – who will be going through a process of learning about and understanding their mistakes.

Your journey is all your own, but sometimes we will collide with other people who are on their own, different journeys, and unfortunate things can happen when we do. That same forgiveness you have just shown yourself after making a mistake, I want you to try to show to others when they make mistakes too.

SOME DAYS IT WILL BE HARD, BUT I WANT YOU TO TRY TO FORGIVE THOSE WHO CAN SOMETIMES HURT YOU. I USED TO THINK THAT FORGIVENESS WAS ALL ABOUT ALLOWING THE PERSON WHO HAD HURT YOU TO MOVE ON, BUT AS I'VE GROWN OLDER I'VE LEARNED THAT FORGIVENESS IS IMPORTANT FOR EVERYONE — NOT JUST THE PERSON YOU ARE FORGIVING, BUT FOR YOU AS WELL. IT'S LIKE A MEDICINE YOU BOTH TAKE THAT CAN HELP YOU GET RID OF THE HURT.

The reason I say that is because there's one more hidden thing that can be the most confusing and annoying thing ever. Sometimes bad things can happen to you and it won't be your fault. Bad things can happen when you make mistakes in life, but bad things will also happen when you've done everything right.

Football is a great example of this. I've experienced games where a bunch of things have gone wrong for my team but somehow, in the dying minutes, we've managed to put it all together and get a winning goal. I've also had games where we've played brilliantly but ended up losing.

You can also make no mistakes and, even so, sometimes things just won't go your way.

WHEN THESE MOMENTS HAPPEN I WANT YOU TO TRY YOUR HARDEST NOT TO BLAME YOURSELF, OR TO TAKE OUT YOUR FRUSTRATION ON THE PEOPLE CLOSE TO YOU. THESE THINGS HAPPEN ALL OF THE TIME, TO ALL OF US.

When I was younger I'd say stuff like 'that's not fair' or 'I must be jinxed' whenever these sorts of situations happened, but as I've got older I've realised it's better for me to take a breath and just accept that these things happen, through nobody's fault. What matters next is how you can go about fixing things — how you bounce back — and I often think that comes from collective responsibility. If a bad thing happens and it's nobody's fault, that doesn't mean no one has to fix it. The best way to move forward is for as many people as possible to link together to create an environment where the bad thing doesn't happen again.

Because no matter what has gone wrong, or how difficult things have been in the past, that doesn't mean things will keep going wrong in the future. There will be moments in life that will be confusing and unfair.

Things can happen out of the blue that make you feel really angry, but understand that they happen to all of us. So it will be important that we all work together to correct it, side by side, pulling in the same direction, so that everything improves. Don't walk away from a mistake and think that life is too hard, or that it's not worth trying, or that it's not your fault and someone else can fix it instead. I genuinely believe that nothing is too hard. Seriously. If you put time and effort and passion into something, then you will get something, no matter how small or strange, out of it as a reward.

THE BEST WAY I CAN DESCRIBE IT IS WHEN A BIG GREY CLOUD APPEARS AND COVERS UP THE SUN DURING A NICE DAY. IT'S NO ONE'S FAULT THE CLOUD APPEARED, AND YOU SHOULD DO WHAT YOU CAN TO GET OUT OF THE RAIN, BUT THE MOST IMPORTANT THING TO REMEMBER IS THAT THE CLOUD WON'T BE THERE FOREVER.

The sun will come out again the next day, and then you can try again with whatever it is you want to do.

1. YOU ARE NOT YOUR MISTAKES

Since all humans make mistakes, and you're a human (unless a really smart cat has decided to open this book!), congratulations! You will make mistakes. You've already made mistakes. You've probably felt bad about those mistakes, but you're not alone.

THINK OF IT THIS WAY: EVERY MISTAKE YOU'VE EVER MADE HAS ALREADY BEEN MADE BY SOMEONE ELSE, AND MANY MORE PEOPLE WILL GO ON TO MAKE THAT SAME MISTAKE IN THE FUTURE. ALL YOU CAN DO IS FIND COMFORT IN KNOWING THAT YOU'RE NOT ALONE, AND THAT YOU CAN ALWAYS LEARN FROM YOUR MISTAKES.

I want you to know that you should never confuse making a mistake for thinking that you ARE a mistake. You're more than the things you've messed up on. You are more than the moments when you feel at your lowest.

What lessons have you learned from making mistakes? I know this might be difficult, but I would like you to write down three mistakes you've made. Then for each one, think about how that mistake taught you to do something different next time. Make sure you write down these lessons next to each mistake too.

Think about how much more you know now that you've been able to reflect on your mistakes. You should be proud of how much you're learning and the opportunities you're having to grow.

2. FORGIVE YOURSELF

You know how I told you to say out loud, **'I am allowed to make mistakes'?** Write out that sentence on a piece of paper using some coloured pencils or pens. Make it into your own work of art, complete with doodles, symbols or other little drawings.

Look at your art whenever you're feeling down about yourself. Repeat what it says in front of the mirror. And remember to try and not be so hard on yourself when those mistakes happen.

3. WORK ON YOUR STACK OF PANCAKES

I know I've been talking about pancakes a lot — are you hungry yet? — but I think it's a really good way to remind ourselves that we are always learning and improving, even when things go badly. What are some things you'd like to keep working on and improving at?

Can you think of a time that you didn't give up after you messed up? What are some things you would've never got better at if you'd quit the first time you made a mistake? Try writing those things down in a list. There are so many things you could add to your list: tying your shoes, riding a bike, learning to read, and on and on! Think about these things as your very own pancake stack. You had to keep trying for things to get better!

ALL ABOUT
THE SQUAD

7

ONE THING I REALLY LIKE ABOUT FOOTBALL IS THAT IT'S A TEAM SPORT.

You don't need much to play it, and you can practise it for hours (and hours) all by yourself. But football truly comes alive when loads of people take part. I've said before that football can be played by anyone, so when everyone gets involved all the emotion, the excitement and the drama is just incredible. Team sports teach you how to work with other people, and you learn about their strengths and weaknesses before deciding how your skills can complement theirs.

(I have a friend who used to hate team sports growing up until their mum made them play Doubles Tennis. They never understood why, until she explained, **'IT'S TO HELP YOU GET ALONG BETTER WITH OTHER PEOPLE – YOU CAN'T WORK AS A TEAM IF YOU CLASH WITH YOUR PARTNER ALL OF THE TIME.'** And, over time, it really helped – my friend slowly learned how to work as part of a team, in tennis, in football, in the classroom and beyond!)

Throughout my life, football has been my gateway to making friends, learning about other people and other cultures, and learning about myself. There were times in my life when I didn't know anyone at school, at Breakfast Club, or the youth club in my area, but the one thing that helped me make friends and overcome any shyness was my love of the team sport. I'd just go up to a group of people while holding a football and ask, 'Do you want to play a game later?'

(If you read my first book, you might remember that this is how I first met my friend Jamie when I was in primary school. He knocked on my door once, holding a football, and asked if anyone was free to play down in the park later, and he's still one of my best friends now!)

I've been on a lot of teams during my life — and I'm not just talking about football teams. There is the team that helps me in my campaigning work, made up of FareShare and other people (some of who you may know, like your parents, school teachers or anyone else who may have supported!) who are working to help get food to those who need it up and down the country. There's my team of friends who make me laugh and who have been there with me through the good times and the bad. There's also my family: me, my mum and my siblings — the very first team I was ever a part of.

I also want to give a shout out to a very special team I'm particularly proud to be a part of. One that you are taking part in right now — it's the team of you who are reading this book!

I feel lucky to be a part of so many brilliant teams. The more time I spend with such amazing, different people, the more I realise something: **when everyone comes together, you can do a lot more than you could ever do on your own.**

When I was younger, that was the reason I enjoyed playing a team sport. But as I've got older, I've realised that **EVERYTHING** is a team sport. Think about it — everything we do is connected to other people.

EVERYTHING WE DO CONTRIBUTES TO A WIDER COMMUNITY AND A BIGGER TEAM, OUTSIDE OF OURSELVES.

That even includes what we think of as 'solo sports'.

Outside of football, I like sports including tennis, golf, Formula 1 and athletics. It might seem that these are all sports that involve just one person, but if you look hard enough, you can see the teamwork at play. My favourite sprinter is Usain Bolt. He was the fastest man on the planet when he ran, and he set world records in the 100m and 200m sprints at the Olympics. But he didn't just wake up one morning and decide to be that fast. He had a team around him, and every person in that team helped him get to that point. A team of running coaches, medics and other sprinters who all contributed to him performing at his best. Even though you only saw the individual at the Olympic final, there was loads of teamwork going on behind the scenes in order to help Usain break world records.

ONE THING I LOVE ABOUT USAIN WAS HE ALWAYS THANKED HIS TEAM AFTER HE WON HIS MEDALS — HE NEVER FORGOT THAT HE WAS PART OF SOMETHING BIGGER, WHERE EVERYONE WAS WORKING TOGETHER TO HELP HIM SUCCEED.

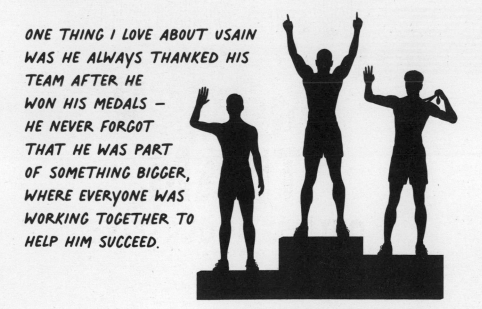

I like films too. (My favourite is *There's Only One Jimmy Grimble!*) Films rely on a lot of teamwork to create, and not just among all of the actors you see on screen. There are stunt people, directors, editors, screenwriters, people who make the special effects, people in charge of the lighting, and even people who sort out the food and drink during filming so that everyone can keep feeling refreshed. Every time you watch a film, look at how many names are featured in the closing credits. It takes hundreds, sometimes thousands of people to make a film. They're all part of a team.

If you ever watch an award show, or a trophy lift or a medal win, you might hear an athlete thank their coaching team, their parents and others before saying,

IT TAKES A VILLAGE TO RAISE A CHILD.

It is one of those sayings that pops up a lot when people want to thank a larger community for some of the success they've achieved. It's something I've carried with me during my journey, as it helps remind me that a lot of the good things I've done in life have been made possible through the help of others. And it's something that you should remember too — you are part of something very special in this world and there are people out there who want the best for you.

EVEN WHEN YOU THINK YOU HAVE NOTHING ELSE, YOU WILL ALWAYS HAVE YOUR LOVED ONES.

In the same way that even individual sports require teamwork, know that you are never alone, no matter how things may seem. *THERE MAY BE TIMES WHERE YOU MIGHT THINK 'NO ONE CARES', OR 'NO ONE UNDERSTANDS', BUT I PROMISE YOU, SOMEONE OUT THERE DOES. EVEN JUST A LITTLE BIT.*

Do you remember I told you earlier on about how I hurt my shoulder a couple of years ago? Well, after that I was pretty down, and I felt very alone. But ultimately it was my brothers and my friends who helped me to feel better. They came to help me. One of them even said to me,

'I DON'T KNOW EXACTLY WHAT YOU'RE GOING THROUGH, BUT YOU'RE IMPORTANT TO ME, SO I'M GOING TO LISTEN AND TRY TO UNDERSTAND MORE.' THAT REALLY MEANT A LOT TO ME.

SO, HOW DO YOU GO ABOUT FINDING YOUR TEAM?

The best teams I have ever been on — football or otherwise — have had loads of good communication, shared interests and transparency. One thing that's incredible about football is that there have been times when I've shared a pitch with people I barely know, but we have been able to communicate through our love of the game. At Manchester United I play next to people who speak English, but also people who speak Spanish, French, Portuguese and other languages. At times it can feel like we don't know how to talk to each other, but we all find a way to work together as a team. We're able to do this because we all have the shared interest of wanting to win football games. And so, as a team, we all learn how to communicate with each other; we all try to learn a few bits of each other's languages — especially words like 'Pass', 'Left', 'Right' and 'Watch out!' — and beyond that we learn how we like to play the game of football. I now have teammates with whom I don't even need to speak to understand what they are thinking; they can communicate with me just by running towards the goal or waving their arms at me.

Football for me is a great 'Universal Language' — you can go anywhere in the world and there will be someone there who loves football, plays football, and understands what football is. There have been times, after my team has won a game, where we're all in the dressing room singing together — people from around the world who want the best for each other, united by their love of football. It always makes me think about how special this game is.

A GOOD TEAM NEVER ALLOWS ANY MEMBER TO FEEL TOO LOW, AND THEY ALWAYS PICK EACH OTHER UP DURING BAD MOMENTS.

There will be times when you disagree, and there will be arguments in your team, but when those moments happen the best way to get through them is by trying to voice your concerns in a way that lets other people around you know that you care more about your friendship than winning an argument. A true teammate tells you things out of love and support, but you need to be aware that there will be people who say things just because they want to argue. The long-term benefits of being with the right people on the right team are far greater than the short term feeling of winning a debate over a small point.

Your team is always going to be bigger than you might think it is at first. It may not always feel this way, but your teacher at school is one of your teammates because they are someone who wants you to do better. For me, my wider teammates include my supporters, in a football sense, but also people who reach out to me and help me on my journey – it could be anyone. Friends of friends, or even people my teachers have recommended.

YOU DON'T ALWAYS HAVE TO BE DIRECTLY CONNECTED TO SOMEONE FOR THEM TO BE YOUR TEAMMATE; IT DOESN'T HAVE TO BE SOMEONE YOU SEE EVERY DAY, AND IT DOESN'T EVEN HAVE TO BE SOMEONE YOU AGREE WITH ALL OF THE TIME.

A teammate is someone who is rooting for you and who shares your values. Anyone who stops and asks, 'Hey, are you ok? How can I help you?' – they are one of your teammates. I consider you, the person reading this, to be my teammate, and I hope that you consider me to be your teammate too!

There will be days where you may feel you are better off doing everything by yourself, but I promise you that you can achieve so much more when you let other people into your life. My friends help keep me anchored to where I am from and all the values I have grown up with. That is something really important to me — where I am in my life now is very different from where I was ten, or even five years ago, but my friends have always been able to help me when I've been struggling. They remind me that the difficult times I have now as a professional footballer are very different from the difficult times I had ten years ago when I was worried I wasn't going to make it. They remind me of who I am when I experience doubts, and they help me remember all of the things I have been through when I start to think the challenges ahead are too much for me to take on.

Your teammates bring out different qualities in you. How I play for England is a bit different from how I play for Manchester United, and how I play for United now is different from how I played when I first joined the senior team, when I was 18 years old. I always ask myself, 'How can I bring the best of me to my team, so my team can do better?' and the

answer is different depending on which team I'm trying to contribute to. In our anti-food-poverty project, I'm not the most knowledgeable person in the room on how to get food to the children who need it, so what I have tried to do is use my connections to bring experts across the food industry together. That's the best way I can contribute to that team.

Different people in your squad will offer you different tools, talents and ways to help you on your journey. Like I said, everything is a team sport, and in the best teams everybody pulls their weight, and everyone pulls in the same direction. Even if we all have slightly different ideas and ways to contribute to it.

ALONE, YOU ARE STRONG BUT WHEN YOU WORK TOGETHER, AS PART OF A TEAM, YOU CAN BE EVEN STRONGER.

WITH THIS BOOK, I WANTED TO SHOW YOU THAT
YOUR VOICE CAN MAKE A DIFFERENCE, AND I WANT
YOU TO REMEMBER THAT ON YOUR JOURNEY TO DO
THIS YOU ARE STRONGER AS PART OF A TEAM.

When used together, everyone's voices will combine to create an
unstoppable force that can do good in this world, like thousands of
droplets of water coming together to make an unstoppable wave. We
needed voices like yours as part of my Child Food Poverty Task Force to
help make the government change its mind — I never could have done
it alone.

And while you're on this journey with your team, there will be moments
when new members join, but also moments when people leave as well.
I've had some really good friends leave my football team and go to other
clubs, or even retire from football. You may have had your friendships
groups change if you've ever moved house or switched schools. It's a little
sad, but try not to get too downbeat about things. Every
friendship you make, every team that you

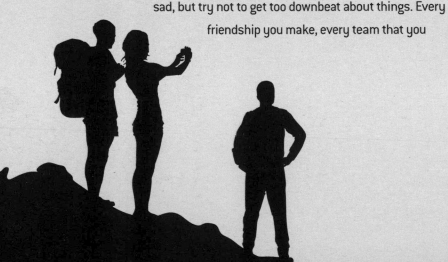

play a part in, serves as a foundation for something even greater down the line. The schoolmates I had when I was in primary school taught me the importance of kindness and looking out for each other, and that is something I have carried with me to secondary school and beyond, even though I don't see them as much now.

THE CHANGE IS OK.

Everyone has their own journey in life, and you're going to learn different things from your friends, and grow up to become different people. Be open to that process and embrace it. You might not have the same circle of friends now that you had five years ago, and that circle may change again another five years from now. You yourself are going to go through changes too. You may start off by using your voice to change one thing, and that journey may lead you on a path to something else.

IT HAPPENED TO ME. EARLIER IN THIS BOOK I SHOWED YOU HOW A LETTER I RECEIVED FROM A FAN CHANGED MY LIFE – SOMETHING SIMILAR MAY HAPPEN TO YOU. NO MATTER HOW IT MIGHT CHANGE, TRY TO MAKE SURE THAT WHOEVER IS IN YOUR TEAM LOVES AND UNDERSTANDS YOU. Make sure your team is a place where you feel comfortable being yourself, where your voice is heard, and that it's a place where you feel comfortable contributing to whatever adventures you may have ahead.

I am a product of my team, and every kind gesture and helping hand from them has contributed to my journey. If I ever worry that the challenges ahead are too much for me, I stop and look to my team, and they show me that there isn't a challenge in the world that I'll have to take on by myself. A challenge may be too big for me to take on alone, but it is never too big for my team.

When you are lost, look to your friends, family, teachers, coaches and other people and they will help show you the way forward. They will remind you of all of the things you have been through together, and let you know there is no reason to be afraid of what will come in the future, because no matter what happens you will not face it alone.

I want you to remember that everything in your life is a team sport. Everything good requires loads of people working together to make it happen.

TOGETHER, WE'RE BRILLIANT AND WE'RE SO MUCH STRONGER THAN WE ARE APART.

1. IT TAKES A VILLAGE

There is a saying spoken by the Zulu people of South Africa: 'Umuntu ngumuntu ngabantu'. Translated into English, it means **'a person exists through their relationships with others'**. We are all connected to each other, and the more we can rely on and give to our neighbours and community members, the more society will work as part of a well-functioning team.

Think about all the people out there who help you in the life you have. There are loads of people helping you every day, including people you have never met. There are farmers who've grown the fruits and vegetables you eat, there are the people who make the electricity work so you can stay warm and dry when it's cold, there are people who've made the clothes you're wearing right now, and people who shipped the things you have in your house across the world to get to you. That's a lot of people who help you in your day, before we even think about the people you know and talk to, like your family members, your friends, and your teachers.

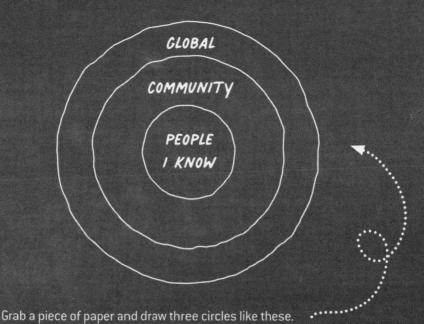

Grab a piece of paper and draw three circles like these.

Write one of the following words or phrases in each circle: **'global'**, **'community'** and **'people I know'.**

Add as many people you can think of to each circle to see how we're all connected!

You might put farmers in 'global', NHS workers in 'community', and your teachers in 'people I know'. If you don't know which circle something goes in – like how far away your food comes from – you can research it and learn more about the teams of people near and far who help your life every day!

2. CHANGING TEAMS, DIFFERENT SEASONS

Make a list of friends and other 'teammates' who you used to know but who moved away, you moved away from, or you just don't see each other any more. What did each person teach you or bring out in you? Maybe your former teacher made you realise how much you like to make art, or your old school friend showed you how important it is to laugh together and be silly when you're feeling sad.

Remember that teams changing is a part of life. What is important is how we remember and value the things our old teammates have given us when we become part of new teams.

BE A
TEAM PLAYER

8

HEY.

IT'S THE FINAL CHAPTER OF THIS BOOK.

HOW ARE YOU DOING?

I always get a bit emotional at this point. There's still so much I want to share, but I'm so glad you've been with me up to now. I hope you've enjoyed reading this book as much as I've enjoyed writing it.

Like I said in the last chapter, now that we've been on this journey together, we're teammates.

I HOPE YOU KNOW THERE ARE LOADS OF PEOPLE OUT THERE WHO HAVE READ THE SAME PAGES AS YOU HAVE. WHO HAVE HELD THE SAME BOOK IN THEIR HANDS. I HOPE YOU THINK ABOUT THEM AS YOUR TEAMMATES, TOO.

You're going to be a part of many different teams in your life and you're going to have some of the most amazing adventures with them. Things you never thought were possible. Things you didn't even know you could do. You're already brilliant, just the way you are, but when you link up with other like-minded people and work towards something together . . .? That's where the magic happens. That's when you all – together – start to be magnificent.

In the last chapter I wanted to show you how amazing it can be to be a part of a team, and in this chapter I want to show you how important it is to be a good team player. To respect the people around you. Working as part of a team is one of the most wonderful things you can experience. I know that when I work in a team I get such a boost: to my mind, my body . . . everything, really. When I work as part of a team I learn how to make things that seem impossible, possible. So before our time is up together, I want to share some advice . . .

I'm not always going to be a professional footballer – there might be a point in my thirties when I decide to stop and leave things for the next generation of players – *BUT I HOPE THAT I'LL ALWAYS BE A GOOD TEAMMATE THROUGHOUT MY ENTIRE LIFE.* This book has been my attempt at passing on some of the things I have learned about being a friend, an ally, and a teammate through the years.

There was once a time in my life when being 'too friendly' was something that was looked down upon. Certain areas I grew up in had a bad reputation, and even innocent questions like 'Have you got the time?' were considered dangerous. Something that you should never respond to.

And while it's true that being on my guard and only looking out for myself may have helped me to survive, I think to truly thrive and live you have to try to participate in a wider group. That requires being a little bit vulnerable at times and trusting other people around you. I'm not going to pretend that trying to do the right thing is going to work 100% of the time, but I don't want you to be discouraged from trying to be kind to others just because something bad has happened in the past. Life can be complicated, but the best way we get through tricky situations is through kindness, honesty and vulnerability, rather than being cruel or withdrawing yourself from the wider community.

Showing a bit of vulnerability – and by that I mean letting others get to know you, the **REAL** you – is important when you want to be a good team player. It can be easy to believe that vulnerability is a negative thing, or that 'letting your guard down' is something you shouldn't do. But the way I see it, how can I expect people to know what I am striving for and how they can help me if I'm not willing to be honest and share my thoughts with them?

> I WOULD REALLY LIKE TO LIVE IN A WORLD WHERE BEING KIND ISN'T THOUGHT OF AS BEING 'WEAK' OR 'NAIVE'. WHERE BEING KIND IS JUST BEING KIND. AND I WOULD LIKE TO LIVE IN A WORLD WHERE PEOPLE CHOOSE TO DO THE RIGHT THING, LIKE STANDING UP FOR WHAT YOU BELIEVE IS RIGHT, LOOKING AFTER THOSE WHO NEED YOU, AND GOING OUT OF YOUR WAY TO LEARN AND SHARE WITH OTHER PEOPLE.

It's not the easiest thing to be open and honest about yourself – both the good bits and the bits that you might not like talking about – but a large part of being in a team, or in any partnership, is being able to trust the people around you. And I think one way of showing people you can be trusted is to first trust them with a little piece of yourself.

Think about it – since you started reading this book you've learned about my favourite shop in my local area, my favourite film and how much I love the Ninja Turtles. I've also talked to you about things that have made me worried in the past, as well as things I'm not so good at – and the mistakes I have made. You now know that before I wrote that letter to the members of parliament, I was afraid of letting people know I didn't grow up with much as a child. I've trusted you with those things because I want you to feel less worried about trusting the people that you care about with your likes, hobbies and vulnerabilities. If we can cause a little chain reaction, where everyone is just a little bit nicer and a little bit more trusting with each other, then we can create a great team that can do loads of good work. You'll understand how to better support your teammates, and they'll understand you better, too.

Within football, I've learned how to be open and how to contribute to something bigger than myself. I've learned a lot about different cultures, different personalities and how different people like to go about certain tasks. When we're learning a new training routine at Manchester United or England, some players like to learn by having things explained to them verbally, while others like to learn by watching someone else do it. There are also players who like to go through the routine themselves, as that is how their brain picks things up. There is no right or wrong way, but only what works best for each person.

ONE GOOD FOOTBALL PLAYER CANNOT WIN EVERY GAME BY THEMSELVES. THEY HAVE TO BE A GOOD TEAM PLAYER AND CONNECT WITH OTHERS ON TOP OF ANY PERSONAL SKILLS THEY MAY HAVE.

Everything I've learned about teamwork on the football pitch has, in turn, taught me that in life there is a place for everyone within your team. They don't always have to speak the same language, come from the same place, or like the same thing for breakfast, but what matters more is how they work with everyone else to achieve a greater goal. And you can achieve those goals by being open and asking loads of questions, then listening to the answers and learning from them. In my team, we try to give space to everyone and make sure that everyone feels comfortable enough to be their true selves.

I always remember the kindness my friends showed me when I was doing my drawings as a child, and I have tried to bring that kindness and understanding to every team I have been on since. Think about it – I know what I know, and my teammates know what they know. What we each know is always going to be a bit different, so when we share our own knowledge with each other – together – we all end up knowing a little bit more.

A good team player always wants to know more. About their teammates. About themselves. And about what they can do to improve both.

A question I am constantly asking myself is:

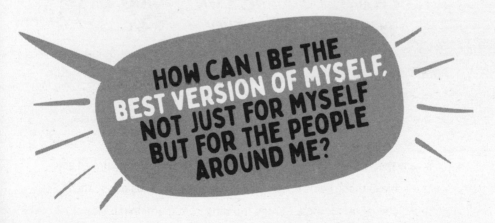

HOW CAN I BE THE BEST VERSION OF MYSELF, NOT JUST FOR MYSELF BUT FOR THE PEOPLE AROUND ME?

WHEN YOU ASK YOURSELF THAT, YOU OPEN YOURSELF UP TO A LOT OF POTENTIAL FOR GROWTH.

There is this word you might hear later in life, which is 'solidarity'. It describes the good feeling between people when they are looking out for each other and working together towards something greater. Solidarity is the word that describes the 'I help you, and you help me' feeling that you may experience from time to time. It's a word I use a lot when I talk to my friends, my family, and other people in my team. I like how it has the word 'solid' in it, to remind you of how powerful a group can be when they all work together.

A good team is full of people who have solidarity with each other. A good team player embraces the different journeys, different backgrounds and different personalities within the group, then works to make the connections between everyone even stronger. You've got to be welcoming to new additions, but also be respectful when people have disagreements or want to leave.

WHEN YOU'RE A GOOD TEAMMATE, YOU'RE SOMEONE WHO PATS YOUR FRIEND ON THE BACK WHEN THEY HAVE DONE WELL AND PICKS THEM UP WHEN THEY'VE STUMBLED. YOU HAVE TO HAVE YOUR FRIEND'S BACK SO THEY CAN HAVE YOURS LATER DOWN THE LINE.

A good teammate understands that even though they can be successful individually, what matters more is making sure everyone in the group is also doing well. I think it's a bit like learning to cook. When you make a good meal for yourself, it's nice, but when you make dinner for someone else and they say 'that was really tasty', it makes you feel even happier! I want to do well not just for myself, but so I can share that success with my friends. I work hard to make sure my mum and my siblings are doing well. And when they are successful, that makes me just as happy as when I win a game of football with England or Manchester United.

Being a good team player can be as simple as saying **'Good job!'** or **'I'm proud of you!'** to someone when things go well. It can be letting the people around you know that you appreciate them. 'We couldn't have done this without you' is a wonderful thing for a person to hear, and I always smile when someone tells me 'I really like that you are here'. Make sure you say good things about your teammates, even when they aren't around to hear them!

WHEN YOUR FRIENDS WIN, YOU WIN, TOO.

WHEN YOUR TEAMMATES WIN, CELEBRATE THEIR SUCCESS JUST AS HARD AS YOUR OWN.

There will be times when your team ends up disagreeing with each other, but there is always a way to avoid a big bust-up. Communication is so important to being a good team player. If you have an issue with someone you care about, know that you are allowed to voice that issue, but I think a lot of fights and arguments come from how people explain their thoughts and feelings to each other. Like I said in the last chapter, a good squad has your best interests at heart, and I think that when you want to voice your disagreement with someone, the most effective way to do that is to come from a place of love – where you want both yourself and the other person to do better – rather than trying to hurt someone else. When I want to tell a friend or someone on my team that I am hurt, I try to do it calmly, and in a way that lets the other person know that I'm coming from a place of concern, rather than anger.

184

I know that a team works better when it's in a positive, healthy environment, so even when things aren't going so well, I try my best to take a moment and make sure I'm communicating my thoughts and feelings in the right way. I like to take a few moments to understand and acknowledge my feelings, and then I make an effort to explain to the other person so they understand where I am coming from. When I play football there are moments when I have missed a chance to score because I tried shooting too early. My coaches often tell me to stop rushing things and to 'take a touch with the ball when you can'. When I take a touch for big chances playing football, it allows me extra time to get my body and mind in the correct place so I can figure out what I need to do next on the pitch.

I think it's important to 'take a touch' for off the field problems too. When things get a bit hectic and there are emotions going all over the place, try not to rush things. Try to 'take a touch' when you can and look inward. If you're feeling angry, ask yourself why. If something is annoying you, try to explore where that feeling is coming from. I don't want you to ever have to rush yourself – you're on your own journey and I want you to take it at a pace that is comfortable for you.

A good team needs 'good vibes' – where everyone is singing the same song, in tune with each other, to perform at their best. But if that positivity comes at one person's expense and there are bottled-up feelings, then that's no good. Communication is a vital part of teamwork, and explaining yourself thoughtfully and clearly, even when things aren't going well, is a very important way to maintain that positivity.

THE WAY I SEE IT, IT COMES BACK TO TRUST. EVEN WHEN YOU DISAGREE WITH PEOPLE IN YOUR TEAM, YOU HAVE TO BE ABLE TO TRUST THEM WITH YOUR FEELINGS AND TRUST THAT THEY WILL RESPECT YOUR OPINIONS BACK IN KIND.

You also have to respect other people in your team when they come to you with their feelings. When you're a good team player you try your best to listen, and you're open to being challenged and asked questions. You want to be able to respect people around you in such a way that you all feel comfortable talking about sensitive topics. It's not easy when someone comes with criticism of you or something you have done, but part of learning is about taking on the feedback others give you. If you are willing to give your friends advice on how they can do better, you have to be willing to take on the advice they give you in return.

I consider myself to be made up of the goodness and kindness of so many people I have shared teams with. I think one of the secrets of being a good teammate is to collect all of that kindness you've received and then try to pay it forward to someone else. It could be anyone: a sibling, a friend, a classmate, a neighbour . . . anyone. When you help someone else, you help spread more good into the world. And when you do that, all sorts of exciting things happen.

At the end of my last book, I told you there are no limits to what you can achieve. Here, I want you to know there are no limits to what you can achieve when you work as part of a team.

STAY CURIOUS, ALWAYS.
ASK AS MANY QUESTIONS AS POSSIBLE
ABOUT THINGS YOU KNOW,
ABOUT THINGS YOU DON'T KNOW,
AND ABOUT THE THINGS YOU ARE
EXCITED TO DISCOVER NEXT.

188

There's also one question that's really, really important to being a team player. In fact, if you go back a little bit, you'll realise that I started this chapter by asking you that question.

One of the most powerful questions you can ask other people – and yourself – is **'How are you doing?'** It's such a simple phrase, but it can be a powerful thing when somebody reaches out and checks in. It's that little reminder that there are people out there who are thinking about you and who have your best interests at heart. I know that when I am in a low mood, a friend asking me 'How are you doing?' is like someone walking into the dark room I'm in and switching on a light. All of a sudden things are a lot clearer. I know that I am not alone and that there is someone out there who is looking out for me.

TRY TO ASK THAT QUESTION TO YOUR FRIENDS A LOT. MAKE THEM CUPS OF TEA. ASK THEM, 'WHAT CAN I DO TO HELP?' CHECK IN. YOU'LL FEEL BETTER YOURSELF WHEN YOU TRY TO HELP MAKE SOMEONE ELSE FEEL BETTER. TRUST ME.

And try to check in on yourself, too. You have to be your own best friend – your own teammate – a lot in your life, so make sure to ask yourself how you're doing. It will be important in the weeks, months and years to come.

We have a lot of work to do if we want to make the world a better place, and I don't want this book to make you feel as if you're in some sort of great race to change the world, all by yourself.

But I want you to take just a small moment to imagine all of the different people who might be holding this book along with you, and realise that they have been reading the same things you have.

NOW IMAGINE ALL OF YOU TOGETHER GOING OUT THERE AND SHARING JUST THE SMALLEST BIT OF ADVICE FROM HERE WITH SOMEONE YOU KNOW.

NOW IMAGINE THEY SHARE SOME OF THAT ADVICE WITH SOMEONE THEY KNOW.

AND THEN THAT PERSON PASSES SOMETHING ELSE ON TO SOMEONE ELSE.

We have a lot of work to do, but never forget how many of us are out there, all ready and waiting to help you change the world, too.

Because that's how we get things done.

TOGETHER.
YOU CAN DO IT.

M.R.

1. STAND UP FOR WHAT YOU BELIEVE IN

There are a lot of things in this world I don't know about.

- I'm not the best cook.
- I get lost a lot when I'm asked to read a map.
- I'm trying to learn Spanish and Italian but sometimes I get my words mixed up.
- I'll even admit that sometimes I meet other footballers and they know parts of the game better than I do.

I don't know everything about everyone in the world around me, nor do I think I will have learned everything there is to know by the time I'm old(er) and my hair is grey.

One thing I do know though – 100% for sure – is that you've got to be kind.

We should be kind to each other as it is the best way to get things done.
We should be kind to each other because it is nice to be nice.
We should be kind to each other because I think it is one of the most
important things you can be.

So keeping kindness in mind, what are some things that you believe in?
What are some things that you believe are important, where you can
show kindness? What are some of the things you can work with others
to achieve?

It can be anything, like the food programme I've helped set up.
Or you could try to stand up for someone when someone else is being
unkind to them or is putting them down?
Or maybe you care about the environment?
Or welcoming people who are new to your area, like immigrants and
refugees?

Grab a piece of paper and write out a table with three columns.

Write 'Things I Care About' at the top of the first column, and underneath that write a cause you think about a lot.

Write 'How Can I Be Kind to Others?' at the top of the second column. Underneath that write some ways you can work towards helping the cause you wrote down.

Write 'How Can I Work with Others?' at the top of the third column. This is the most important bit. Here you need to write down ways you can work with other people who also care about the cause.

You can repeat this exercise with as many causes as you want!

My columns for my anti-food-poverty project looked like this:

Things I Care About	How Can I Be Kind to Others?	How Can I Work with Others?
I care about children on free school meals.	I want to be kind to others by donating and writing to people in government about it.	I can work with others on this cause by asking them to do the same as me.

At the end of this exercise, you could end up with loads of different ways that you can use kindness to work with others to take care of causes close to your heart. And that can be the start of something special.

2. COMMUNICATION IS THE NAME OF THE GAME

In this chapter, we learned a lot about why communication is so important when you're part of a team.

I want you to take a piece of paper and split it in half this time.

On one side, write down ways that you like to communicate and learn. Do you prefer to have things explained to you verbally? Do you like to learn by watching someone else do it? Do you learn best by yourself? Or do you prefer to learn in a mixture of all three ways?

On the other side of the paper, I want you to write down the names of people you love, and then have a think about how they like to communicate. This bit is a little tricky! Just because you respond well to one type of communication, it doesn't mean that everyone around you does as well.

Think about your teachers at school. Do you have a favourite? If so, why? Think about how they communicate with you in class. Are they loud? Quiet? Do they give you words of encouragement when things go well? Or do they prefer to give you words of encouragement when things aren't so good, so you can get back up on your feet?

When I play football, I prefer it when my coaches tell me to keep my head up when things are bad, rather than tell me I am brilliant when things are already good. But that's not the same for everyone.

Part of communicating is explaining how and why you communicate. It's also asking questions to the people around you, to understand how they like to communicate too!

AND REMEMBER: IT'S IMPORTANT TO COMMUNICATE WITH YOURSELF, ESPECIALLY WHEN YOU'RE HAVING SOME HARD FEELINGS! THE MORE YOU CAN ASK YOURSELF HOW YOU'RE DOING AND UNDERSTAND YOUR OWN EMOTIONS, THE BETTER YOU'LL BE ABLE TO UNDERSTAND WHERE OTHER PEOPLE ARE COMING FROM.

YOUR
INDIVIDUAL
ACTIONS
ADD UP TO A
COLLECTIVE
IMPACT!

HOW CAN I HELP?

ABOUT THE AUTHORS AND CONTRIBUTOR

Marcus Rashford MBE

Marcus Rashford MBE is Manchester United's iconic number 10 and an England International footballer.

During the lockdown imposed due to the COVID-19 pandemic, Marcus teamed up with the food distribution charity FareShare to cover the free school meal deficit for vulnerable children across the UK, raising in excess of 20 million pounds. Marcus successfully lobbied the British Government to U-turn policy around the free food voucher programme – a campaign that has been deemed the quickest turnaround of government policy in the history of British politics – so that 1.3 million vulnerable children continued to have access to food supplies whilst schools were closed during the pandemic.

In response to Marcus's End Child Food Poverty campaign, the British Government committed £400 million to support vulnerable children across the UK, supporting 1.7 million children for the next 12 months. In October 2020, he was appointed MBE in the Queen's Birthday Honours. Marcus has committed himself to combating child poverty in the UK and his book *You Are a Champion: How to Be the Best You Can Be* is an inspiring guide for children about reaching their full potential.

Carl Anka

Carl Anka is a London-born journalist and broadcaster who likes his tea with milk and one sugar. He has written for the *BBC*, *The Guardian*, *VICE*, *NME*, *GQ* and *BuzzFeed* among other publications online and in print, and specialises in writing about pop culture, video games, films and football. Currently a reporter for sports media group *The Athletic*, covering Manchester United, he is the host of the *Talk of the Devils* podcast and is scared of talking on the phone.

Along with Marcus Rashford, Carl is the co-writer of *You Are a Champion: How to Be the Best You Can Be* – a positive and inspiring guide for life for young readers.

Shannon Weber

Shannon Weber, Ph.D is the Director of Digital Learning at The Body Is Not An Apology, a digital media and education company grounded in the concept of radical self-love. She is also the author of three books on social justice and equality, most recently the children's book *Activists Assemble: We Are All Equal!*

THE MARCUS RASHFORD BOOK CLUB

Look out for the Marcus Rashford Book Club logo — it's on books Marcus thinks you'll love!

MARCUS RASHFORD BOOKCLUB CHOICE

A brilliantly illustrated, laugh-out-loud, wacky adventure through time!

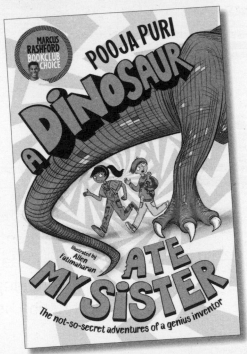

Marcus says: 'The perfect story to escape into and find adventure. Pooja is super talented and I'm a big fan!'

Marcus says: 'Fun, engaging, action-packed — I would have loved this book as a child!'

Meet the Dream Defenders! They're on a mission to banish your worries while you sleep!

TOM PERCIVAL

'I would have loved this book as a child' Marcus Rashford MBE

MARCUS RASHFORD BOOKCLUB CHOICE

Silas AND THE **Marvellous Misfits**

A fantastic DREAM DEFENDERS adventure!

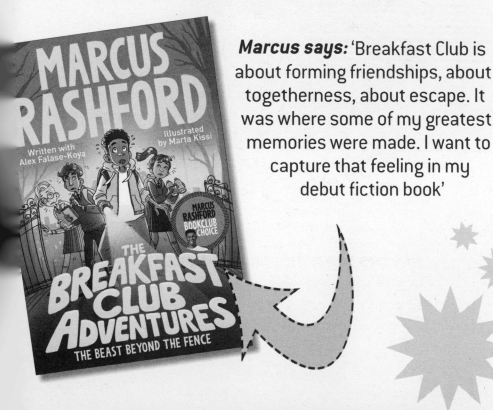

MARCUS RASHFORD

Illustrated by Marta Kissi

Written with Alex Falase-Koya

MARCUS RASHFORD BOOKCLUB CHOICE

THE **BREAKFAST CLUB ADVENTURES**

THE BEAST BEYOND THE FENCE

Marcus says: 'Breakfast Club is about forming friendships, about togetherness, about escape. It was where some of my greatest memories were made. I want to capture that feeling in my debut fiction book'

THE MARCUS RASHFORD
BOOK CLUB

The Marcus Rashford Book Club is a collaboration between Marcus Rashford MBE and Macmillan Children's Books, helping children aged 8–12 to develop literacy as a life skill and a love of reading. Two books will be chosen each year by Marcus and the Macmillan team, one in summer and another in the autumn, with the mission to increase children's access to books outside of school. The book club will feature an exciting selection of titles, which aim to make every child feel supported, represented and empowered.

The book club launched in June 2021, with the fully illustrated, laugh-out-loud, time-travel adventure, *A Dinosaur Ate My Sister* by Pooja Puri, illustrated by Allen Fatimaharan, followed by *Silas and the Marvellous Misfits* by Tom Percival, an action-packed, fully-illustrated adventure that shows kids the joy of being themselves. Marcus's own book, *The Breakfast Club Adventures: The Beast Beyond the Fence*, written with Alex Falase-Koya, is the third book in the club. Copies of these books will be available in shops, and to ensure all children have access to them, free copies will also be distributed to support under-privileged and vulnerable children across the UK.

Don't miss Marcus Rashford's first positive and inspiring guide for life!

The Number One Bestseller

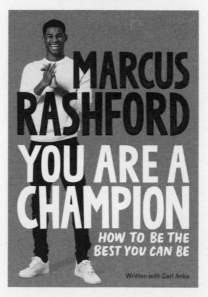

'I want to show you how you can be a champion in almost anything you put your mind to.'

Marcus Rashford MBE is famous worldwide for his skills both on and off the pitch – but before he was a Manchester United and England footballer, and long before he started his inspiring work to end child food poverty, he was just an ordinary kid from Wythenshawe, South Manchester. Now the nation's favourite footballer wants to show YOU how to achieve your dreams, in this positive and inspiring guide for life.

Don't miss Marcus Rashford's first fiction book for kids!

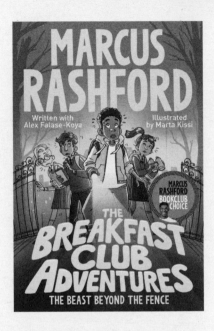

There's something strange going on at school . . .

When twelve-year-old Marcus kicks his favourite football over the school fence, he knows he's never getting it back. Nothing that goes over that wall ever comes comes back.

But when Marcus gets a mysterious note inviting him to join The Breakfast Club Investigators he is soon pulled into an exciting adventure to solve the mystery, along with his new mates Stacey, Lise and Asim!

As they uncover one surprising club after another, the Breakfast Club Investigators start to realize that things aren't as they seem, and there might be something strange lurking just beyond the fence . . .